THAT OLD OVERLAND STAGECOACHING

Eva Jolene Boyd

Republic of Texas Press
an imprint of
Wordware Publishing, Inc.

Library of Congress Cataloging-in-Publication Data

Boyd, Eva Jolene
  --That old overland stagecoaching / by Eva Jolene Boyd.
      p.   cm.
  Includes bibliographical references (p.   ).
  ISBN 1-55622-250-5
  1. Coaching--Texas--History.   2. Coaching--Southwestern States
  --History.   Title.
  HE5748.O7B69   1991
  388.3'228'0976--dc20   91-18719
                                                       CIP

1506 Capital Avenue
Plano, Texas 75074

Printed in the United States of America

ISBN 1-55622-250-5
10 9 8 7 6 5 4 3 2 1
9209

All inquiries for volume purchases of this book should be addressed to
Wordware Publishing, Inc., at the above address. Telephone inquiries may be
made by calling:

(214) 423-0090

"... the driver sent the weird music of his bugle winding over the grassy solitudes, and presently we detected a low hut or two in the distance. Then the rattling of the coach, the clatter of our six horses' hoofs, and the driver's crisp commands, awoke to a louder and stronger emphasis; and we went sweeping down on the station at our smartest speed. It was fascinating — that old Overland stagecoaching."

(Mark Twain, *Roughing It*)

Dedicated To

"Honey"

and

Jerry

Contents

Acknowledgments

As with any book of this nature, the author does not write it without the help of many others. First and foremost, God has always been there, prodding me, giving me quiet encouragement when I was frustrated with the manuscript's progress. Also, my mother and brother (and to both this book is dedicated) often cheered me when I was down.

Many thanks to Wayne R. Austerman, author of the excellent book on the San Antonio-El Paso Road, *Sharps Rifles and Spanish Mules*, who so kindly waded through some of his own notes and pictures to aid me in particular sources; to John Neilson of the Fort Concho Museum Library, who found time to look for pictures; to Douglas McChristian, who sent me his treatise on military protection in the vicinity of Fort Davis; to the librarians at Butt-Holdsworth Library in Kerrville for their seemingly unending patience in searching for interlibrary loans; to all the librarians and archivists who have helped in this regard. And to William Latham, who searched the El Paso library files for me to find the photo of the Butterfield station.

I've got to thank Frank Lively, former editor of *Texas Highways Magazine*, who gave my proposed book a plug in the magazine with my article on the Butterfield Stage Road, which led to this publication. I especially want to thank all the authors whose own works were invaluable sources; to the Conklings, whose three-volume work is an absolutely priceless source for historians on this subject. Thanks, too, to Robert A. Clark of the Arthur H. Clark Company, for his assistance and consent to use material from the Conkling book.

And, certainly not leastly, to Vardra McBee McGinnis, an ancestor of mine who drove stagecoaches in East Texas in the 1850s—I believe he was standing behind me all the time—and to all the drivers and passengers, and the men and women who worked the lonely stations, the soldiers who guarded them, and to the John Butterfields and James Birches, all of whom made this story possible.

Eva Jolene Boyd

Introduction

In 1659 Sir William Dugdale "set forwards toward London by Coventre coach" and public transportation hasn't been the same since.[1]

It is doubtful that this English nobleman, whose account is said to be the first documented description of public coach travel in England, ever gave a thought to the ancestors of the vehicle in which he rode to London town, or to the five hundred year occupation of England by the Romans. And it is highly unlikely that either early English coaches or Roman occupation entered the minds of travelers who journeyed by stagecoach across the American West in the mid- to late-1800s. Yet, both had an impact upon this time in our history, one of the most romantic periods from the frontier era.

Whatever the evils of their occupation, the Romans left behind a legacy of hundreds of miles of good paved roads, an efficient postal system, and the first functional public coaches used in the country before they withdrew from England early in the fifth century A.D. The ancestor of what is familiar to us as the stagecoach was nothing more than a modified Briton chariot. The Romans merely lengthened the platform and installed a seat for two passengers. They also built fifteen forts in northern England, each a day's journey apart, and connected them with paved roads. With a postal station at each fort, the Romans used fast carriages to carry dispatches and military commanders from one post to another. Later they built vehicles to haul baggage, and in time installed seats to carry passengers as well and roofs to keep out the rain. As traveling in such conveyances became vogue, the wagons were ornamented and equipped with such luxuries as curtains and upholstered seats.

After the Romans left, the roads were allowed to deteriorate. Mail had to be carried by mounted messengers because wheeled vehicles could no longer be pulled over the wretched highways. The development of the stagecoach in England went into limbo for nearly a thousand years.

By the sixteenth century, some improvements had been made on the roads so that work began again on the development of passenger vehicles. The first coach to be manufactured in Britain may have been one built in 1555 for the Earl of Rutland. Coach construction on a large scale appears to have occurred during the reign of Queen Elizabeth I (1558-1603). By the end of the eighteenth century, English-built coaches were considered to be among the finest in the world and were widely exported.

But, if there was a single factor in the improvement of public transportation, it was the government subsidy. When the Crown began awarding contracts to operators, the whole range of passenger service improved, including roads, coaches, service, and facilities.

Staging on the eastern seaboard of America paralleled to some extent that of the mother country. English vehicles were used in the "Colonies," but American wheelwrights were building coaches as early as 1687, mostly copying the English and French models.

The evolution of the stagecoach in America did not really begin until after the Revolutionary War when the government banned the import of British products. Then, American ingenuity took over, resulting in some rather strange contraptions early on. The first primitive public coaches resembled the covered wagon, the "prairie schooner" of the American West a half-century later. Unpadded, backless seats were built across the wagon beds.

Late eighteenth century "stage waggons" were improved in that they had a hard superstructure with a canvas roof and curtains over the windows that could be lowered in inclement weather. There were no doors, however; one had to enter through the open front. Nor was there any space for baggage.

If you couldn't stash it under your seat, you didn't need to bring it anyway.

There was one major improvement, however; the designers had done away with the steel springs and suspended the body on thoroughbraces, two lengths of rawhide mounted on steel stanchions, thus returning to a system a couple of centuries old. Thoroughbraces had their own discomforting peculiarities to be sure, but their use would make possible two thousand mile stage rides across the West.

Next to the thoroughbraces, the most notable improvement in the design of the public stagecoach was, literally, from the box to the egg. Whether by accident or design, someone discovered that an egg-shaped body placed upon thoroughbraces produces a rocking motion instead of the head-snapping vertical jolts produced by conventional springs. An 1802 advertisement for the Annapolis and Georgetown Mail Stage showed a more refined, egg-shaped vehicle with a rear "boot" to hold luggage. The egg shape remained in use over the next couple of decades, its major drawback, however, being that extra passengers or luggage could not be carried on the severely curved roof.[2]

By this time Lewis Downing and J. Stephen Abbot had established an enviable reputation for building some of the finest vehicles on the road. Downing, at age 21 and with only $60 in his pocket, had opened a wheelwright shop in 1813 in Concord, New Hampshire. He was no stranger to the trade; his father-in-law was a stage driver and the Downing family operated a carriage business in nearby Lexington. In just three years he had gained such prominence in building top quality wagons and chaises, that he had to enlarge his factory and take on more employees to handle his orders. Ten years later he hired 22-year-old J. Stephen Abbot, a journeyman coach-body builder from Salem, Massachusetts.

In 1828 Downing and Abbot became full partners in their burgeoning business. Only the year before they had designed a vehicle that would turn the industry on its ear. The beautifully crafted, sturdy Concord coach would become the Model-T of the nineteenth century.

A page from an Abbot catalog, ca. 1850-1860, showing the various models of stagecoaches and other wagons built by the company. The hack wagon shown was lighter than the famed Concord coach and, similar to the Celerity, was used throughout the Southwest by John Butterfield. (Courtesy New Hampshire Historical Society)

A Concord was a magnificent vehicle when it rolled out of the factory, with gold leafing, scrollwork, russet leather upholstery, side lamps, perhaps a landscape painted on the doors. A coach like this, "loaded," cost the customer around $1,400. It could also be ordered plain for many hundreds less.

Lewis Downing was his own quality-control department. A master craftsman himself, he tolerated nothing but the best from his employees, many of them imported from Scotland and England. If a product did not meet his standards, it was completely destroyed so that no part of it could be used again.[3]

Particular attention was paid to the wheels as these were usually the first objects to break on the road. All pieces were fitted together so tightly that no bolts or screws were needed. Only the best woods were used and iron was found only in the axles and bearings, axle irons, door handles, hinges, and bracings. Western Concords were heavier than their eastern counterparts, weighing 3,000 pounds, and were capable of carrying a two ton load.

The last of the old stagemen, William and George Bannings, could not sing enough praises of the Concord. "With trim decking and panels of the clearest poplar," they wrote, "and with stout frame of well-seasoned ash, this body, in all of its tri-dimensional curves, fairly held itself together by sheer virtue of scientific design and master joinery, for very little iron was used . . . . "[4]

The use of thoroughbraces had been one of the most significant improvements in the evolution of the stagecoach. Conventional steel springs had several drawbacks: they broke readily, were unbearable over anything but the smoothest of roads, and were especially hard on the teams. When a vehicle hit an obstacle, such as a rock or a hole, the resulting shock wave traveled through the traces to the animals' shoulders, ultimately shortening their working life span. Thoroughbraces, on the other hand, absorbed most of the shock.

Coaches riding on thoroughbraces produced a curious motion, described by some as that of a rocking chair. Mark

Twain called it "an imposing cradle on wheels."[5] Many travelers, strangely enough, complained of seasickness.

The passenger seats, which rested on coiled steel springs, were cushioned by horsehair and covered with the finest calf leather. Hand straps were located on the inside next to the windows for passengers to hold on to in rough going. Anyone sitting in the middle, however, had only the press of his or her companions on either side to hold him in his seat.

Before a Concord left the factory, the body glistened under several coats of paint, each coat rubbed with pumice and the whole covered with spar varnish. Coaches were finished to the customers' needs and painted accordingly, but most were red with yellow wheels and matching red striping. The noted nineteenth century artist John Burgum was employed at the factory to decorate the doors. These, too, were specified by the buyer but were usually of landscapes and people. Each coach bore a serial number and the factory kept close tabs on the vehicle throughout its career.

The Concord coaches were not the only passenger vehicles on the roads by any means. The Albany Coach, manufactured by James Goold & Company of Albany, New York, was introduced in the 1820s. The Eaton, Gilbert and Company of Troy, New York, built stagecoaches which, like the Albanys and Concords, were known by the name of the town in which they were manufactured. Founded in 1823, this firm is said to have originated putting "dicky seats" on the roof for extra passengers. The Albany and Troy coaches were well respected for their quality of construction, but it is the Concord which has become synonymous with stagecoaching in the West.

Around the same time that the stagecoach for the West was being designed, Texans were winning their independence from Mexico, thus opening up a vast new land to settlement. In another dozen years, certain events would occur that would expand the United States all the way to the Pacific and test to the fullest the inventiveness of men like Abbot and Downing. It would become America's golden age of stagecoaching.

Notes, Introduction

1. Alexander Andrews, "Coaching," 677, quoted in Oscar Osburn Winther, *The Transportation Frontier*, 59.
2. Ibid., 4-5. There are several good books which detail the history of coaching both in England and the United States. Among them are, Clarence P. Hornung, *Wheels Across America*; Oliver W. Holmes and Peter T. Rohrbach, *Stagecoach East*, which covers coaching in the eastern United States from the Colonial period to the Civil War, including many illustrations showing the various stages of the coach's development; Ralph Moody, *Stagecoach West*, which traces the history of wheeled transportation back to the Stone Age; David Mountfield, *The Coaching Age*, examines coaching history in England and in continental Europe; and Richard F. Palmer, *The "Old Line Mail,"* which traces in detail the history of staging in New York State.
3. Holmes and Rohrbach, *Stagecoach East*, 100. Several sources accounted, in varying degrees, the Abbot-Downing and coach building stories. I found the best for detail to be: Roscoe P. Conkling and Margaret B. Conkling, *The Butterfield Overland Mail, 1857-1869*, 377-383; S. Blackwell Duncan, "The Legendary Concords," *The American West*, 16-17, 61-62; Richard Dunlop, *Wheels West, 1590-1900*, 132-136; Nick Eggenhofer, *Wagons, Mules and Men*, 160-161 (includes excellent detailed drawings of coach's assembly and undercarriage); Clarence P. Hornung, *Wheels Across America*, 40-41; Ralph Moody, *Stagecoach West*, 11-19; and Oscar Osburn Winther, *The Transportation Frontier*, 60-61.
4. Capt. William Banning and George Hugh Banning, *Six Horses*, 24.
5. Mark Twain, *Roughing It*, 5.

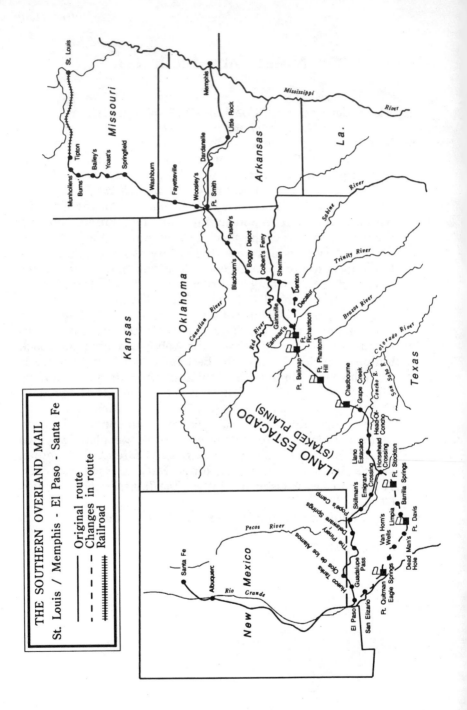

THE SOUTHERN OVERLAND MAIL
St. Louis / Memphis - El Paso - Santa Fe

Original route
Changes in route
Railroad

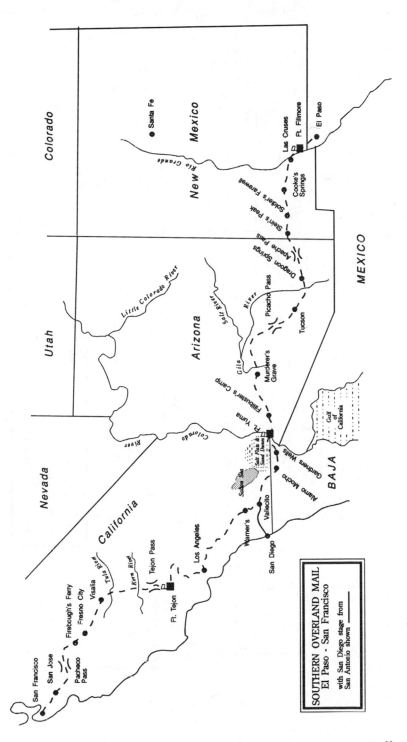

SOUTHERN OVERLAND MAIL
El Paso - San Francisco

with San Diego stage from
San Antonio shown ——

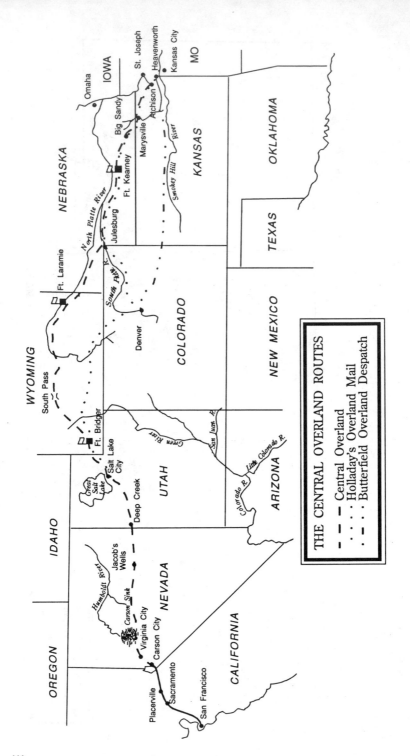

THE CENTRAL OVERLAND ROUTES

— — Central Overland
· · · · Holladay's Overland Mail
—·—·— Butterfield Overland Despatch

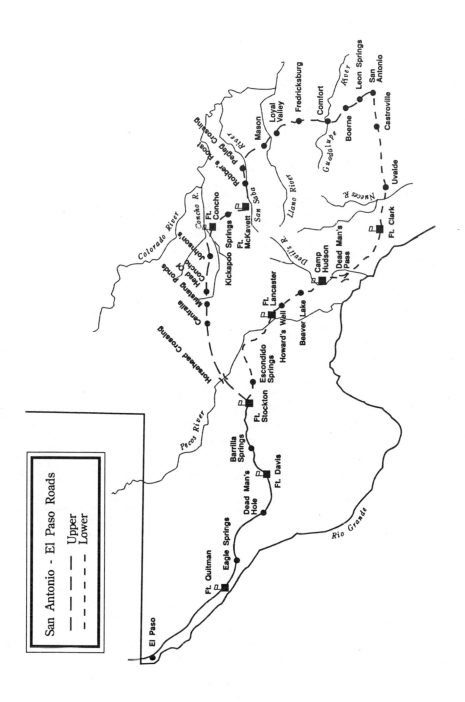

San Antonio - El Paso Roads

Upper
Lower

El Paso

Ft. Quitman

Eagle Springs

Dead Man's Hole

Ft. Davis

Barrilla Springs

Pecos River

Ft. Stockton

Escondido Springs

Horsehead Crossing

Centralia

Mustang Ponds

Head of Concho

Ft. Johnson's

Colorado River

Concho R.

Kickapoo Springs

Ft. Concho

Ft. McKavett

San Saba River

Robber's Roost

Pegleg Crossing

Mason

Loyal Valley

Fredericksburg

Comfort

Leon Springs

San Antonio

Boerne

Castroville

Guadalupe River

Llano River

Nueces R.

Uvalde

Ft. Clark

Dead Man's Pass

Camp Hudson

Devil's R.

Ft. Lancaster

Howard's Well

Beaver Lake

Rio Grande

CHAPTER ONE
"The Natural Roads of Texas"

*"Ten years ago there was only one
apology of a stage line in the State."*[1]

This jab in the San Antonio *Herald* in February of 1858 said quite a lot about the progress that had been made in Texas in the previous decade. By then, public transportation had gone from "one apology of a stage line" to a fine system of stage lines, including the longest stage route in the world.

Some semblance of a mail system had been inaugurated in December of 1835 when the provisional government established a postal department and a few routes. The following December, the First Texas Congress of the new republic created a general post office department.

The early postal system sorely lacked in efficiency. Service on most routes was rarely more frequent than weekly or bi-monthly with the mail carried on mule or horseback. Animals ran off, taking the mail with them. Mail sacks weren't always protected from the weather or else fell into ditches and often arrived at their destination an illegible mass of wet pulp.[2]

Still, from this primitive beginning, there were 3,786 miles of mail roads in operation in Texas by 1846 shortly after being annexed into the Union.[3]

The exact year when stagecoaches began running in Texas is obscure, but a historical marker in front of the Rice Stagecoach Inn near Crockett states that this was a stopping place for coaches as early as 1838. In 1839 a stage line was established by Starke-Burgess to run twice weekly between Houston and Austin. The company advertised that the trip took three days, one way, and cost twenty-five cents a mile.[4]

This was an exorbitant amount and must have been a "First Class" or "Bad Weather" rate. Most of the lines charged ten cents a mile; but if it had been raining or looked like it was going to, the stage operator could raise, even double, the basic fare. For the privilege of going first class, a passenger paid for a VIP status; that is, he wasn't required to help pull coaches out of mud holes or ditches. The drivers were always assured of having more than enough helping hands, however; few travelers could afford double rates on most overnight trips.[5]

Much of the early agrestic travel in Texas was a far cry from the relatively comfortable sojourns of later experiences. Consider Dr. Ferdinand Roemer, a German lawyer and paleontologist who spent two years in the mid-1840s examining the country's mineral resources for future emigrants. He boarded a stagecoach for Houston at a New Braunfels hotel in April of 1846 and described the bi-weekly service between Houston and San Antonio as having recently been established. Roemer's trip would take 3½ days with nightly layovers at inns or hotels and cost $20, including his trunk.[6]

The coach in which he traveled was little more than a carriage frame "on which a square box without springs was fastened." His seat was suspended by straps which broke soon after leaving New Braunfels, forcing Roemer to sit on his trunk.[7]

At Gonzales the stage connected with the coach from Austin and several passengers were added for the trip to Houston. There were now nine souls occupying the vehicle, ". . . creating a very crowded condition." It was a situation that reflected the times as Roemer continued, "extra coaches, which are also unknown throughout America, were not to be found here."[8]

Shortly after leaving Washington [-on-the-Brazos], a thunderstorm erupted and, as the wagon was not covered, all were drenched, save for the lady traveler who enjoyed the chivalry extended by her male companions who took turns covering her with an umbrella. To make matters worse, the road was soon turned to a quagmire and the men were ordered by the driver to walk. Roemer was at least encouraged by the proprietor of the inn where they stayed that night with news that "good covered coaches for the entire system had been ordered from the northern states."[9]

Stage routes expanded in the eastern half of the state during the early 1850s and, although service improved, continued to suffer from frontier hazards and unpleasantries. Not all accounts by travelers were negative, however. An English woman on a sightseeing jaunt of East Texas in 1855 found her experiences pleasing.

Despite four days and nights of hard going, she was none the worse for wear. The coaches were "so good and so well appointed," Amelia Murray wrote, "that, although the roads were very rough and dusty, we had no cause to be frightened, except in passing the loose plank bridges, most of them with no pretence [sic] of a rail to prevent vehicles and horses from going over the sides . . . these coaches have such fine horses, and such admirable drivers, that I never travelled at night with such confidence as through the wild forests and natural roads of Texas."[10]

Julius Froebel's experiences, on the other hand, ran the gamut of adventure and tribulation, all told with a singular wit. Of a journey to Indianola from San Antonio in 1853, he wrote:

"The stage-coach journey . . . was most peculiar, and would probably have excited the ill humour of a less-tried traveller; but it only awakened merriment in me and my companions. I paid, if I mistake not, 12½ dollars for my seat, for which price I secured the privilege of walking three-fourths of the distance—about 160 English miles—and was obliged to help to pull the coach out of the mud-holes in which it should stick fast . . . ." Froebel had purchased a new suit of clothes in San Antonio for his return to "civilized life," but was forced to discard them at Indianola because of the mud and grime.[11]

He made the trip in reverse a few months later and indicated that the roads were in "no better state than on my journey down in July, and similar tragi-comic occurrences happened now as then. The first night I was obliged to run before the carriage for a considerable distance with a stearine candle in my hand, through a deep marsh, in order to find out the road . . . ."[12]

Although travelers continued to suffer "tragi-comic" circumstances, Texas was well served by stage lines by the 1850s. Every major town had a service and several became connecting stops. Nacogdoches, for example, was the center of two stage lines, one westward to San Antonio and Houston and another east to Louisiana. Navasota, another important junction, was served by the Bates and Black, and Northwest Texas Lines which linked Navasota with such distant points as Shreveport, San Antonio, and Fort Worth.

Most roads led to San Antonio. Like the hub of a wheel, old Bexar was the center of stage routes branching out in all directions. Probably the longest route served by Texas points up to 1850 was the Overland Stage Line which operated between San Antonio and Little Rock, Arkansas. This line ran through Salado, another major crossroads. Coach traffic was particularly heavy through Bell County, the largest operator being the Sawyer and Compton Line which connected Waco and Austin. This line may have enjoyed the longest staging career in the country as it continued to operate until 1881.[13]

By the early 1850s, coaches were rolling as far west as Fredericksburg. But beyond that point lay hundreds of miles of no-man's land, at least no men's but the Indians', offering little incentive to settle in the area.

Since Texas' victory for independence over Mexico in 1836, first one thing and then another had slowed the republic's westward expansion. During the decade of sovereignty, there simply hadn't been enough money in the treasury to blaze new roads or protect settlers on the frontier. Then, in 1846, war came once again to the border with Mexico.

The old stagecoach at Manchaca Springs, near Austin (Texas). Note the hack in the rear. Date unknown. (Courtesy Texas State Archives)

In 1848 two unrelated events brought about a sudden and dramatic change. First, gold was discovered in a stream in California, and just two weeks later, the signing of the Treaty of Guadalupe Hidalgo signaled the end of hostilities with Mexico and opened up the entire Southwest to American settlement. By the following year, nearly one out of every 20 California-bound emigrants leaving the east coast by sea landed at Texas ports and struck the long trail west.[14]

That same year, Lieutenants William H. C. Whiting and William F. Smith, of the Corps of Topographical Engineers, set out from San Antonio to scout a road to Fort Bliss, near the Mexican city of El Paso, more than six hundred miles away. They followed, for the most part, a route surveyed the year before by John C. Hays and Captain Samuel Highsmith but returned by a more southerly path and regarded it as the better of the two because of its numerous permanent springs.

This latter route, alternately called the Whiting and Smith, or Lower Road, coursed west from San Antonio to Las Moras Springs [at present Brackettville], northwestward to the Devil's River, Live Oak Creek near the Pecos River, then westward to the Apache [Davis] Mountains, and on to El Paso along the Rio Grande.

In mid-September of 1850 Henry Skillman took it upon himself to carry the first mail over the Lower Road. The following year he signed a contract for the San Antonio-Santa Fe mail and that December advertised the addition of "carriages" for passengers. The fare over the dangerous route, one way, was $125.00. Despite the perils of the road, and Wayne Austerman lists no fewer than five Indian attacks on coaches between January 1852 and April of 1853, the lure of gold outweighed the dangers and forty-niners continued to run the gauntlet across West Texas.[15]

The mail contracts changed hands several times between 1851 and 1857; from Henry Skillman, to David Wasson, to George Giddings, each fined or punished at one time or another by the postmaster general for failure to render mail service on schedule. It said something about the times, however, that anyone sitting safe behind a desk a thousand miles away could understand the complexity of sending stagecoaches into an untamed frontier.

Still, El Pasoans had a right to complain about the mail service. They did, and their voices were heard all the way to Washington. Louder still were the voices of the 75,000 Californians who signed a petition in 1856 demanding an overland postal service, then shipped the voluminous package to Congress. The following February, $200,000 was appropriated for a mail route between El Paso and Fort Yuma. It was only a temporary solution, but the wheels that would permanently link the east and west had been set in motion.

Notes, Chapter One

1. San Antonio *Herald*, 6 February 1858.
2. Joann V. Pappas, Editor, "The Irregular Mail of the Texas Republic," *Star of the Republic Museum Notes*, Vol. IV, No. 4, Summer 1980.
3. W. L. Newsom, "The Postal System of the Republic of Texas," *The Southwestern Historical Quarterly*, Vol. XX, No. 2, October 1916, 111.
4. Kathryn Turner Carter, *Stagecoach Inns of Texas*, 91. Carter's book is an excellent source for the history of the East Texas inns and hotels that served as stage stops.
5. Rupert Norval Richardson, *Texas, the Lone Star State*, 159; Carter, 9, taken from Harry Starnes, "Century-old Taverns, Where Stage Coaches Halted Are Yet Standing," *San Antonio Express*, 22 November 1936.
6. Dr. Ferdinand Roemer, *Texas*, 291.
7. Ibid., 292.
8. Ibid., 294.
9. Ibid., 297-298.
10. Amelia M. Murray, *Letters From the United States, Cuba and Canada*, 298.
11. Julius Froebel, *Seven Years' Travel in Central America, Northern Mexico, and the Far West of the United States*, 427.
12. Ibid., 432-433.
13. Carter, *Stagecoach Inns of Texas*, 190.
14. Wayne R. Austerman, *Sharps Rifles and Spanish Mules*, 4. Austerman's book is an excellent source for a thorough background on all aspects of the San Antonio-El Paso Road. It is a must for history buffs as well as the serious historian.
15. Ibid., 315-316.
16. Froebel, *Seven Years' Travel*, 417.

CHAPTER TWO

"Your Panama steamers might as well lie up . . ."

". . . Four-horse stages cannot be driven from San Francisco to Memphis in twenty-five days—nor in forty days—nor at all."[1]

Poor John Butterfield. First he won the mail contract on a route he didn't bid on and then he had to go about getting the line in operation amidst predictions of failure and a poisonous civil war of words between the North and the South.

The same could be said about James Birch. He lost the mail contract he bid on—to Butterfield—and won a route that suffered from almost constant Indian depredations and the indignity of being described as going "from no place through nothing to nowhere."[2]

The story begins long before Birch and Butterfield, however. It began when those little yellow nuggets were found at Sutter's Mill, followed within days of the treaty between the United States and Mexico. With a nation suddenly on the move, now was the time for men of grit.

Henry Skillman, born in New Jersey about 1814, was one of those men. More than six feet tall, sporting long sandy hair and beard, dressing in buckskin, and adorned with an assortment of Bowie knives and revolvers, Skillman was the epitome of the Texian frontiersman. He had ridden the Santa Fe Trail as a courier in 1842, drove freight wagons over the Santa Fe-

Chihuahua trade route, and distinguished himself in the Mexican War where he served as a scout. He won the San Antonio-Santa Fe mail contract in 1850, after initiating service to El Paso on his own the previous year, and lost it in 1854 when he was unable to provide adequate passenger service.[3]

David Wasson, an eastern stageman and partner of John Butterfield, was awarded the contract after Skillman but discovered that trying to operate a stage line by proxy over that particular route was more than he could handle. Wasson gratefully transferred his contract to George Giddings that October. Thus began the career of one of the most tragic characters in the era of stagecoaching.[4]

When George H. Giddings and his brother James arrived in Texas in February of 1846, their family name was already well established in the new frontier, a long way from Susquehanna County, Pennsylvania. One brother, Giles, had died at San Jacinto ten years earlier while serving in Sam Houston's army. Another brother, Jabez (for whom the town of Giddings in Lee County, Texas, is named), was a prominent lawyer and resided in Brenham when his siblings arrived. Two more brothers, DeWitt and Frank, would also join the immigration of the Giddings clan to Texas.[5]

George, twenty-two years old when he arrived, studied law for a while then served as district and county clerks until the onset of the Mexican War called him to join a volunteers battalion. After the war he tried surveying and other odd jobs, but found the West more challenging and wound up in San Antonio driving freight wagons to Mexico for a mercantile firm. When the owners decided to sell out a short time later, George Giddings invested his savings and bought the business, including the store in San Antonio and a trading post at distant El Paso. This set of circumstances would lead to his involvement in the mail and passenger stage service between San Antonio and San Diego, California, and more heartache than he could have imagined at the time. By 1855, 673 miles of the 1,637 total miles of mail coach road in Texas belonged to George Giddings.[6]

The lives of John Butterfield and James Birch followed far different paths than did Skillman's and Giddings' on their way to becoming legends in the Southwest. Both men, native New Englanders, had served their apprenticeships with stage lines. But, whereas Butterfield remained in his native New York while building his fortunes, James Birch could not resist heading for California to look for gold. What he found was far more tangible.

Born in Rhode Island in 1828, Birch was barely twenty-one years old when he arrived in California. He soon decided, however, that his gold mine did not lie in a streambed; he thought the claims too crowded. Instead, he bought four scrawny mustangs for next to nothing and an old ranch wagon to which he nailed enough boards to seat 24 passengers. He then charged prospectors $32, or two ounces of gold dust if they didn't have the cash, to haul them 30 miles, one-way, from Sacramento to their claims at Mormon Island.[7]

The enterprise had its inaugural run in September of 1849 and, despite the exorbitant rate—some twenty times the rate of similar mileage back east—the receipts from the first run more than repaid his initial investment. Soon Birch was able to order new Concord coaches, buy good horses, and improve the roads. Within four years he had built the largest staging enterprise in the state and amassed a sizable fortune. By 1853 he was president of the California Stage Company.[8]

Still only in his twenties, Birch retired as head of the company and took his fortune back east where he built a seaside estate at Swansea, Massachusetts, for his young bride. The motives for his returning to the east coast are not entirely clear, but it may have been that he wanted to catch a much larger fish than what he had in California. At any rate, he would become a worthy rival for another New Englander who would also build an empire from scratch.

John Butterfield was born November 18, 1801, on his father's farm in Albany County, New York. When he was six, his father took him to Albany to see the new wonder of the world, Robert Fulton's steamboat *Clermont*. If young Butterfield was impressed, the marvel did nothing to sway

11

him from his first love—horses and coaches. On his trips to the capital city, he would hang about the stables and stage stations and tradition has it that he learned to blow a coach horn during these visits.

With the lure of the post roads and fast horses in his blood, Butterfield went to Albany at the age of nineteen and got a job with the staging firm of Asa Sprague and Aaron Thorpe. Jason Parker, proprietor of the Old Line Mail based in Utica, hired the young man as a driver and runner, whose job it was to lure passengers away from competing stage lines and canal boats. He did his duties so well, it wasn't long before his reputation both as a runner and a reinsman was well regarded throughout New England.[9]

JOHN BUTTERFIELD.

Photo courtesy of Library of Congress

SPECIAL INSTRUCTIONS.

In order to carry out this undertaking, it is necessary that the following Instructions be strictly observed by all Employés of the Company.

TO CONDUCTORS, AGENTS, DRIVERS & EMPLOYÉS.

1.—It is expected that all employés of the Company will be at their posts at all times, in order to guard and protect the property of the Company. Have teams harnessed in ample time, and ready to proceed without delay or confusion. Where the coaches are changed, have the teams hitched to them in time. Teams should be hitched together and led to or from the stable to the coach, so that no delay can occur by their running away. All employés will assist the Driver in watering and changing teams in all cases, to save time.

2.—When a stage is seriously detained by accident or otherwise, the Conductor or Driver will have the same noted on way bill and note book, and report fully to the Superintendent at first station the nature and cause of such delay.

3.—Conductors should never lose sight of the mails for a moment, or leave them, except in charge of the driver or some other employé of the Company, who will guard them till his return. This rule must not be deviated from under *any circumstances.* They will also report to the Superintendent in all cases if Drivers abuse or mis-manage their teams, or in any way neglect or refuse to do their duty.

4.—The time of all employés is expected to be at the disposal of the Company's Agents, in all cases, at stations where they may be laying over. Their time belongs exclusively to the Company ; they will therefore be always ready for duty

5.—None but the Company's Superintendents or Agents who have written permission, are authorised to make or contract debts, give notes, due bills, or any obligations on account of the Company.

6.—Conductors and Drivers will be very particular, and not allow the Company's property to be abused, or neglect to report to the proper parties the repairs required.

7.—You will be particular to see that the mails are protected from the wet, and kept safe from injury of every kind while in your possession, in your division, and you will be held responsible for the safe delivery at the end of your route, or point of destination, of all mails and other property in your charge.

8.—The Company will not at present transport any *through* extra baggage, freights, or parcels of any description. All employés are cautioned against receiving such matter in any shape or manner, except such local business of this nature, from place to place, as will be done according to the instructions and prices to be given by the different Superintendents. You will not fail to see that all parcels, boxes or bundles carried on the stage, shall be entered on the way bill, with amount of freight to be charged, and you will be held responsible for the safe delivery, at point of destination, of all such packages. The Agent will see that the charges are paid, and articles receipted for at time of delivery. No money, jewelry, bank notes, or valuables of any nature, will be allowed to be carried under any circumstances whatever.

9.—All Superintendents, Agents, Conductors and Drivers will see particularly that every passenger shall have their names entered on the way-bill at point of departure ; that their fare shall be paid in advance, and the amount entered on way-bill as paid to point of destination. No Conductor or Agent must allow any stage to leave his station without personally comparing the way-bill with the passengers, and knowing that they agree. Each Station Agent will be required to note the time of arrival and departure of each stage at his station, both on the way-bill and on a book kept for that purpose, giving the Driver and Conductor's name and cause of delay, if any has occurred.

10.—Superintendents will report to the President and Treasurer of the Company, and to each other, the names of the persons authorised to receipt fare on way-bill. No others than those named by them will be allowed to receipt fare.

11.—The rates of fare will, for the present, be as follows : between the Pacific Railroad terminus and San Francisco, and between Memphis and San Francisco, either way, through tickets, $200. Local fares between Fort Smith and Fort Yuma not less than 10 cents per mile for the distance traveled. Between Fort Yuma and San Francisco, and between Fort Smith and the Railroad terminus, the rate of fare will be published by the Superintendents of those divisions.

12.—The meals and provisions for passengers are at their own expense, over- and above the regular fare. The Company intend, as soon as possible, to have suitable meals at proper places prepared for passengers at a moderate cost.

13.—Each passenger will be allowed baggage not exceeding 40 lbs. in any case.

14.—Passengers stopping from one stage to another, can only do so at their own risk as to the Company being able to carry them on a following stage. In cases of this nature, the Conductor or Agent at the place where they leave the stage, will endorse on the way-bill opposite their name, " Stopped over at —————." And on the way-bill of the stage in which the passenger continues his journey, the entry of his name will be made with the remark, " Stopped over from stage of the ————— (giving the date). Fare paid to ————— on way-bill of ————— (date) from————— (name the place.)"

15.—All employés are expected to show proper respect to and treat passengers and the public with civility, as well as to use every exertion for the comfort and convenience of passengers.

16.—Agents, Conductors, Drivers and all employés will follow strictly all instructions that may be received from time to time from the Superintendents of their respective divisions.

17.—Any transactions of a disreputable nature will be sufficient cause for the discharge of any person from the employ of the Company.

18.—INDIANS. A good look-out should be kept for Indians. No intercourse should be had with them, but let them alone ; by no means annoy or wrong them. At all times an efficient guard should be kept, and such guard should always be *ready* for any emergency.

19.—It is expected of every employé that he will further the interests of the Company by every means in his power, more especially by living on good terms with all his fellow-employés, by avoiding quarrels and disagreements of every kind and nature with all parties, and by the strictest attention of each and every one to his duties.

M. L. KENYON, *San Francisco, Cal.*
HUGH CROCKER, *Fort Smith, Ark.*
JAMES GLOVER, *El Paso, Texas* } *Superintendents.*
WM. BUCKLEY, *Fort Yuma, Cal.*
GILES HAWLEY, *Tucson, Arizona*
HENRY BATES, *Fort Belknap, Texas,*

JOHN BUTTERFIELD,
President.

239c42

13

No. 1] [Sep. 16th, 1858.

OVERLAND MAIL COMPANY.

THROUGH TIME SCHEDULE BETWEEN

ST. LOUIS, MO., MEMPHIS, TENN. } & SAN FRANCISCO, CAL.

GOING WEST.

LEAVE.	DAYS.	Hour.	Distance, Place to Place.	Time allowed.	Av'ge Miles per Hour.
St. Louis, Mo., & Memphis, Tenn. }	Every Monday & Thursday,	8.00 A.M	Miles.	No. Hours	
P. R. R. Terminus, "	" Monday & Thursday,	6.00 P.M	160	10	16
Springfield, "	" Wednesday & Saturday	7.45 A.M	143	37¾	3 7/9
Fayetteville, "	" Thursday & Sunday,	10.15 A.M	100	26½	3 7/9
Fort Smith, Ark.	" Friday & Monday,	3.30 A.M	65	17¼	3 7/9
Sherman, Texas	" Sunday & Wednesday,	12.30 A.M	205	45	4½
Fort Belknap. "	" Monday & Thursday,	9.00 A.M	146½	32½	4½
Fort Chadbourn, "	" Tuesday & Friday,	3.15 P.M	136	30¼	4½
Pecos River, (Em. Crossing.)	" Thursday & Sunday,	3.45 A.M	165	36½	4½
El Paso,	" Saturday & Tuesday,	11.00 A.M	248½	55¼	4½
Soldier's Farewell	" Sunday & Wednesday,	8.30 P.M	150	33½	4½
Tucson, Arizona	" Tuesday & Friday,	1.30 P.M	184½	41	4½
Gila River,* "	" Wednesday & Saturday	9.00 P.M	141	31½	4½
Fort Yuma, Cal.	" Friday & Monday,	3.00 A.M	135	30	4½
San Bernardino "	" Saturday & Tuesday,	11.00 P.M	200	44	4½
Ft. Tejon, (Via Los Angeles.)	" Monday & Thursday,	7.30 A.M	150	32½	4½
Visalia, "	" Tuesday & Friday,	11.30 A.M	127	28	4½
Firebaugh's Ferry, "	" Wednesday & Saturday	5.30 A.M	82	18	4½
(Arrive) San Francisco,	" Thursday & Sunday,	8.30 A.M	163	27	6

GOING EAST.

LEAVE.	DAYS.	Hour.	Distance, Place to Place.	Time allowed.	Av'ge Miles per Hour.
San Francisco, Cal.	Every Monday & Thursday,	8.00 A.M	Miles.	No. Hours	
Firebaugh's Ferry, "	" Tuesday & Friday,	11.00 A.M	163	27	6
Visalia, "	" Wednesday & Saturday,	5.00 A.M	82	18	4½
Ft.Tejon, (Via Los Angeles)	" Thursday & Sunday,	9.00 A.M	127	28	4½
San Bernardino, "	" Friday & Monday,	5.30 P.M	150	32½	4½
Fort Yuma, "	" Sunday & Wednesday,	1.30 P.M	200	44	4½
Gila River,* Arizona	" Monday & Thursday,	7.30 P.M	135	30	4½
Tucson, "	" Wednesday & Saturday	3.00 A.M	141	31½	4½
Soldier's Farewell,	" Thursday & Sunday,	8.00 P.M	184½	41	4½
El Paso, Tex.	" Saturday & Tuesday,	5.30 A.M	150	33½	4½
Pecos River, (Em. Crossing.)	" Monday & Thursday	12.45 P.M	248½	55¼	4½
Fort Chadbourn, "	" Wednesday & Saturday	1.15 A.M	165	36½	4½
Fort Belknap, "	" Thursday & Sunday,	7.30 A.M	136	30¼	4½
Sherman, "	" Friday & Monday,	4.00 P.M	146½	32½	4½
Fort Smith, Ark.	" Sunday & Wednesday,	1.00 P.M	205	45	4½
Fayetteville, Mo.	" Monday, & Thursday,	6.15 A.M	65	17¼	3 7/9
Springfield, "	" Tuesday & Friday,	8.45 A.M	100	26½	3 7/9
P. R. R. Terminus, "	" Wednesday & Saturday	10.30 P.M	143	37¾	3 7/9
(Arrive) St. Louis, Mo., & Memphis, Tenn. }	" Thursday & Sunday,		160	10	16

This Schedule may not be exact—Superintendents, Agents, Station-men, Conductors, Drivers and all employees are particularly directed to use every possible exertion to get the Stages through in quick time, even though they may be ahead of this time.

If they are behind this time, it will be necessary to urge the animals on to the highest speed that they can be driven without injury.

Remember that no allowance is made in the time for ferries, changing teams, &c. It is therefore necessary that each driver increase his speed over the average per hour enough to gain the necessary time for meals, changing teams, crossing ferries, &c.

Every person in the Company's employ will always bear in mind that each minute of time is of importance. If each driver on the route loses fifteen (15) minutes, it would make a total loss of time, on the entire route, of twenty-five (25) hours, or, more than one day. If each one loses ten (10) minutes it would make a total loss of sixteen and one half (16½) hours, or, the best part of a day.

On the contrary, if each driver gains that amount of time, it leaves a margin of time against accidents and extra delays.

All hands will see the great necessity of promptness and dispatch: every minute of time is valuable as the Company are under heavy forfeit if the mail is behind time.

Conductors must note the hour and date of departure from Stations, the causes of delay, if any, and all particulars. They must also report the same fully to their respective Superintendents.

* The Station referred to on Gila River, is 40 miles west of Maricopa Wells.

JOHN BUTTERFIELD.
Pres't.

Time Schedule - according to Conkling & Conkling, the original of this schedule was carried by James G. Geggs, a Butterfield employee.

Butterfield hoarded his earnings until he was able to buy a horse and a two-seat chaise, which he used to begin a livery business of his own. He married Malinda Harriet Baker in 1822 and the couple opened a boarding house while John maintained his thriving livery service. Butterfield became such an astute businessman that he eventually owned a controlling interest in several New York stage lines. In 1849 he organized the Butterfield and Wasson Express Company and, in 1850, merged with two other firms, Wells & Company, and Livingston & Fargo, to form the American Express Company.[10]

Meanwhile, as the west coast swelled with new settlers and towns, there was an increasing need for a quicker mail and passenger link with the east. Congress took up the issue and began to argue where to put it, how much to spend on it, and whether such a service was necessary in the first place. After all, semimonthly steamer service between New York and California already existed, one route by way of the Isthmus of Panama and another across Tehuantepec, Mexico. The former route involved a 2,000 mile voyage between New York and Aspinwall, the Atlantic port on the Isthmus, a rail trip of 47 miles across the neck of land to Panama, then another voyage of some 3,000 miles to San Francisco. The trip averaged three and a half to four weeks by steamer.

There was also a land route, a monthly mail between Sacramento and Salt Lake City, where it connected with another carrier to Independence, Missouri; but the mails took two months that way and there were no provisions for passenger service.

The Thirty-Second Congress (1852-1853) focused its attention on a railroad, but that would take longer than those on the west coast cared to wait. So the wheels of bureaucracy continued to drag until 1856 when that petition of 75,000 irate Californians was shipped east. Then James Buchanan took the president's office the following March and appointed Tennessean Aaron V. Brown as postmaster general, setting the stage for the era of Butterfield and Birch.

By April 20 Brown was ready to advertise for bids on a new overland route. Nine proposals were received; John Butterfield and his associates bid on three of them and James Birch on one. All of Butterfield's bids called for a line over the "central" route, from St. Louis and/or Memphis to San Francisco by way of Albuquerque, New Mexico Territory. James Birch's single bid called for a more southerly track, from Memphis, through Little Rock, and then across Texas by way of Gainesville and Fort Chadbourne, the Pecos River, and the Guadalupe and Hueco Mountains to El Paso. From there the route would use the old emigrant road to Fort Yuma, and on to San Francisco.[11]

Only one other bid called for a southern route, that from James Glover; the remaining proposals were over the northern or central routes. When the contract was finally awarded, the repercussions were felt all the way from the Potomac River to the Rio Grande.[12]

The first shock came on June 22 when James Birch was awarded a route that was not even among those proposed. The mail was to leave San Antonio, Texas, and San Diego, California, on the ninth of each month, beginning in July, the one-way trip to be made in thirty days or less, and called for appropriations of $149,800 per annum.

Birch actually signed the contract on June 12 and, disappointed though he may have been, had already set things in motion by the time the award was made public. He appointed Isaiah C. Woods as general superintendent and the experienced George Giddings as an agent in San Antonio. He then sent agent James Mason to San Antonio with orders to buy stock and equipment before boarding a mail steamer for San Diego.

While Birch's men set about getting the line ready to roll in time, non-Texans railed against the action. An editorial in the New York *Daily Times* on the 25th accused the postmaster general of favoritism and called the extreme southern route one ". . . least of all adapted to serve the public interest . . . ."

"It is hard to believe that the president and his cabinet would willingly lend themselves to so fraudulent . . . a scheme . . . ."[13]

Needless to say, the contract was met with unbridled enthusiasm in southern quarters, particularly in Texas. The San Antonio *Herald*, that ardent champion of the mail route that linked its city with the west coast, ran this editorial on August 4, 1857:

"The selection has, of course been made the subject of acrimonious comment in Northern journals, as though it had been made for the purpose of influencing the selection of a Southern line for the railroad, merely because it is Southern; as though some duty had been violated and wrong done, because a Northern route for the mails was not taken, because it is Northern . . . ."[14]

At least one northerner praised the selection, however. Rhode Islander John R. Bartlett, the commissioner on the 1850 U.S.-Mexico boundary survey, testified that the route "presents more advantages for a great national highway than any yet discovered, to California."[15]

The first mail under the new contract left San Antonio on the appointed date by horseback, possibly because the new coaches had not yet arrived, as far as El Paso where it was transferred to a coach on August 7.

On the western end, Birch saw the first eastbound mail on its way, then boarded the steamer *Sonora* on August 20 for Panama. There, passengers and cargo transferred to the Panama Railroad for the four-hour trip across the isthmus to Aspinwall where they boarded the luxury steamer *Central America* on September 3 for the last leg to New York. Nine days later, the ship foundered in a storm off the South Carolina coast and went down. More than 400 passengers and crew were lost, including James Birch.[16]

When the first California mail arrived in San Antonio on September 9, a month after leaving the west coast, the September 10 *Herald* reflected the delight of the city's residents. "The trip was made from El Paso to this place in ten days and a half . . . no difficulty with the Indians on the route . . . the mail road has been well marked out, stations established, and relays will soon be arranged. Captain Henry Skillman has been detached upon the San Diego part of the route. It is indeed gratifying to see the contractors on this long and dangerous route, displaying so much energy, in speeding intelligence from the Pacific to the Gulf of Mexico."[17]

It didn't take long for word to reach emigrants headed for California. The San Antonio *Herald* in mid-November reported a full load of passengers on the stage from Indianola and that "many others are on their way up, many of them strangers looking at the country."[18] Included in the number were two men appointed by Birch's widow to see to the continuance of the line.

The furor raised over the San Antonio-San Diego deal paled considerably when the $600,000 contract for the prime route was awarded on September 16.[19] In spite of the fact that none of John Butterfield's bids indicated a route through Texas, he was given the contract for the route bid on by James Birch, that is, crossing the Red River near Preston and arching southwesterly across the state to El Paso. The Civil War almost began then and there, more than three years before Fort Sumter was fired upon.

It was no secret that northerners favored the northern route, which bore west from St. Louis to Independence, then along the North Fork of the Platte River to Fort Laramie, over the South Pass of the Rocky Mountains to Fort Bridger, Salt Lake City, then to follow a branch of the Oregon Trail for Placerville and Sacramento. They would have even compromised and gone for the middle, or central, route, which, from St. Louis, followed the Canadian River, thence to Albuquerque and over the military road to California.

But, their reaction to the southern, or "Ox-Bow" route as the New York press unflatteringly dubbed it, was one of outrage. The Chicago *Tribune* called the contract "one of the greatest swindles ever perpetrated upon the country by the slave-holders."[20]

Brown, whose hometown was Memphis, Tennessee, defended his decision, arguing that the southern route would be "safe, comfortable, and certain during every season of the year."[21] And he had a point. Though better watered and cooler during the summer months, the northern track would have been impassable at times in the winter. Even the central route was less favored for the same reason.

The pros and cons generally ran along sectional and party lines. For instance, Senator Robert A. Toombs of Georgia defended the contract. "The Butterfield route was not selected as a southern route or a northern route, but as a United States route, upon the cheapest, best, and nearest way of getting the mails through."[22]

But, many editorialists adamantly refused to believe that the proposed schedule could be kept, claiming that stage-coaches could not be driven from San Francisco to Memphis at all. "Human ingenuity, cannot devise a plan for such an unheard-of achievement . . . . It never has been done. It never will be done."[23]

While protests continued to fly and sections of the country exchanged insulting barbs, John Butterfield went about build-ing his stage line. Although he had a year to accomplish the feat, it was a monumental task.

The entire route had to be surveyed; some roads had to be built and existing ones improved; unfordable streams had to be bridged. Almost half of the 2,700-mile plus route lay through uninhabited wilderness. Two hundred stations were planned, ideally placing them every ten to twelve miles apart. (Only 140 would be ready when Butterfield's stages began rolling.) They had to be built, stocked, and manned; wells had to be dug where underground water was available, and provi-sions made for hauling it where it was not.

While Butterfield's men worked westward from the east-ern half of the route, Californians worked eastward from San Francisco. The San Francisco *Call* reported on February 4, 1858, that a vanguard of the stage line, two wagons, had arrived in San Bernardino and were on their way to Fort Yuma. ". . . they are delighted with the route," reported the *Call*, "and when the stage line gets in full blast, your Panama steamers might as well lie up—perhaps."[24]

John Butterfield and his associates in the venture began with a capital stock of some $2 million. It was estimated that half that amount was expended in preparing the line for operation, mainly in purchasing 1,000 horses, 500 mules, 800 sets of harness, and some 500 coaches and utility wagons.

To facilitate the running of the stage line, the route was divided into two sections, one east and one west of El Paso, the approximate halfway point. The route was then further divided into nine divisions counting eastward from San Francisco. Each section had a general superintendent and each division would have an agent with a superintendent over him.

Texans living along the proposed route between the Red River and Fort Belknap were ecstatic about the coming stage line. Jack County officials built thirty miles of new road and had them ready two weeks before the first coaches arrived. Neighboring Young County also appropriated funds to cut a new road to Fort Belknap. West of that post, the road builders followed existing military and exploration trails, but most of them were little more than scratches in the ground.

Already under fire from the north, some of the stage line's loudest opposition came from other Texans. As early as March of 1858, the San Antonio *Herald* gleefully predicted the opposing line's failure, while extolling the service to and from its city. Especially since the most recent mail from San Diego had arrived in just 23½ days.

"From all we can learn on the subject," the editorialists wrote, "we think it doubtful whether the [Butterfield] contract will ever be put into operation, from the difficulties of the route, whilst should it fail there is every probability from the favorable nature of the El Paso route, that we should have from this city to San Diego an increase of service either to a Semi-weekly or Weekly Mail."[25]

San Antonians were justified in their concern about the Butterfield line. With the latter taking over the route from El Paso westward, they feared that their line would suffer from any curtailment of its services, especially with a cut in funds. "Retrenchment" became the rallying cry for verbal attack.

As the predictions of calamity and failure continued to echo from the north, and from South Texas, Butterfield proceeded to get his line into operation. Final test runs were made over the entire route and a schedule established, the first of which called for the mail to leave the eastern termini, St. Louis and Memphis, and the western end, San Francisco, at 8:00 A.M. every Monday and Thursday. The mail would travel by train 160 miles from St. Louis to Tipton, Missouri, at the time, the western terminus of the railroad. The mails from St. Louis and Memphis would converge at Little Rock, Arkansas.

Butterfield gave these final instructions to all his employees:

> *"Remember boys, nothing on God's earth*
> *must stop the United States Mail!"*[26]

Then, on the afternoon of September 16, John Butterfield, attired in a long linen duster and "wide-awake hat," personally carried the first mail bags from the train at Tipton to a waiting Concord and handed them to his son, John, Jr., in the driver's box. He made one last, quick inspection of the shiny new coach, tightened a harness strap here, checked a wheel there, then reached up to shake his son's hand before taking a seat inside.

The conductor cried, "All Aboard!," gave one short blast on his coach horn, and at 6:15 P.M., only minutes behind schedule, the first westbound coach was on its way.[27]

Meanwhile, the first eastbound was already on the road, having rolled out of San Francisco's Portsmouth Square with "Tate" Kenyon at the reins, more than 24 hours ahead of schedule.[28]

A young reporter for the New York *Herald* named Waterman Ormsby was the only through passenger booked on the inaugural westbound stage. Four days out of St. Louis, while the coach waited for a relay team, he took time to write a letter to the newspaper which set the tone for the journey.

"There seemed to be a sort of catching enthusiasm about the whole trip, which excited more interest . . . than I ever supposed could be mustered out of the bare fact of a common coach travelling over a common road, with a common mailbag and a few common people inside. But the occasion made them all uncommon, and I soon got so that I would willingly go without my dinner for the privilege of helping along that mail a quarter of an hour."[29]

It was an uncommon time.

Notes, Chapter Two

1. Sacramento *Union*, 3 September 1857. In Mae Helene Bacon Boggs, *My Playhouse Was A Concord Coach*, 281.
2. Capt. William Banning and George Hugh Banning, *Six Horses*, 108.
3. Robert N. Mullin, *Stagecoach Pioneers of the Southwest*, 2-5; Waterman L. Ormsby, *The Butterfield Overland Mail*, 68.
4. Mullin, 6; Wayne R. Austerman, *Sharps Rifles and Spanish Mules*, 58.
5. Austerman, 66; Emmie Giddings W. Mahon andChester V. Kielman, "George H. Giddings and the San Antonio-San Diego Mail Line," *The Southwestern Historical Quarterly*, Vol. LXI, No. 2, October 1957, 220-221; and Walter P. Webb and Joe Bailey Carroll, Eds., *The Handbook of Texas*, I: 686-687.
6. Austerman, 64, 66, 77; Mahon and Kielman, 222-225; and Mullin, 6-9. The noticeable difference in the mileage of post roads per Austerman in 1855 and the 3,786 miles in existence in 1846 may be that most of the mail carried in the early years was by horse or mule back. The lower total miles in 1855 represented coach mail roads only.
7. Oscar Osburn Winther, *Via Western Express & Stagecoach*, 7.
8. Ibid., 11; Mullin, 11.
9. Richard F. Palmer, *The "Old Line Mail,"* 67.
10. Roscoe P. Conkling and Margaret B. Conkling, *The Butterfield Overland Mail, 1857-1869*, I: 31; and Palmer, 67-68.
11. Conkling and Conkling, II: 366-367.
12. Ibid.
13. New York *Daily Times*, 25 June 1857.
14. San Antonio *Herald*, 4 August 1857.
15. Ibid., 9 September 1857.
16. Judy Conrad, "Final Voyage," *American History Illustrated*, 58-65, 72.
17. San Antonio *Herald*, 10 September 1857.
18. Ibid., 19 November 1857.
19. Conkling and Conkling go into considerable detail of the awarding and resulting repercussions over the Overland Mail contract, I: 103-120. Another excellent source is LeRoy R. Hafen, *The Overland Mail, 1849-1869*, 79-92.

20. LeRoy R. Hafen, *The Overland Mail, 1849-1869*, quoted in, 92, from Curtis Nettels, *Missouri Historical Review*, xviii, 529.
21. Winther, 113.
22. Hafen, 123.
23. Sacramento *Union*, 3 September 1857. In Mae Helene Bacon Boggs, *My Playhouse Was A Concord Coach*, 281; and Banning, 144.
24. San Francisco *Call*, 4 February 1858; quoted in Ralph Moody, *Stagecoach West*, 103.
25. San Antonio *Herald*, 23 March 1858.
26. Moody, 108. Moody states that Butterfield inspected the whole line himself; but I could not find any other source where Butterfield ever traveled over the route any further west than Fort Smith, Arkansas, or Sherman, Texas.
27. Conkling and Conkling, 163.
28. There seems to be a difference of opinion as to the exact time the eastbound coach departed San Francisco. LeRoy R. Hafen, *The Overland Mail*, 94, stated that the west- and eastbound coaches left their respective terminals at the same time. The editors of Waterman Ormsby's letters, *The Butterfield Overland Mail*, xii-xiii, quoted a piece from the San Francisco *Bulletin* of 14 September 1858 that the "through mail to Memphis and St. Louis starts from this city at one o'clock tomorrow morning . . . ." Conkling and Conkling, however, stated that the first eastbound coach "dashed out of Portsmouth Square at ten minutes past midnight of Tuesday, September 14th." [I:164]. Considering where the west- and eastbound coaches met, and allowing for speed, the former date is probably correct.
29. Ormsby, 16-17.

CHAPTER THREE
"An American vehicle
is never full . . . ."

*"To make excellent jam; squeeze
six or eight women, now-a-days,
into a common stage-coach."*[1]

Had the author of an article that appeared in the Omaha *Herald* sometime in 1877 received his commandments from a divine source, he probably would not have come up with a better set of rules.

Under the title, "Hints for Plains Travelers," the writer offered the following among his ironclad suggestions:

"Don't smoke a strong pipe inside especially in the morning, spit on the leeward side of the coach . . . Don't swear, nor lop over on your neighbor when sleeping . . . Don't ask how far it is to the next station until you get there . . . Never attempt to fire a gun or pistol while on the road; it may frighten the team . . . Don't discuss politics or religion, nor point out places on the road where horrible murders have been committed, if delicate women are among the passengers . . . Don't grease your hair before starting or dust will stick there in sufficient quantities to make a respectable 'tater' patch . . . ."[2]

But the reams of letters, journals, and articles from that era indicate that most passengers were either ignorant of any golden rules or felt that such articles of discipline did not apply to them. However, circumstances often dictated the event, and the stories that come from the pens of stagecoach riders across the Southwest rival the most imaginative novelist.

Take the seating arrangements. The engineering genius and design of the vehicle notwithstanding, one has to wonder if stage agents harbored a secret sadism in forcing nine adults of assorted sizes into an area about the size of a modern compact automobile. (A Concord, for instance, was about five feet wide and slightly under eight feet long.)

The Cadillac of the frontier, a western Concord stagecoach. Unlike the simplistic design on this Wells Fargo coach, some customers ordered elaborate landscapes or portraits on their doors. The usual colors, as with this one displayed in the Wells Fargo History Museum in San Francisco, were red bodies and yellow wheels with black striping, and black leather on the curtains, and front and rear boots.

No one described the situation better than Raphael Pumpelly, who boarded a westbound Butterfield stagecoach in October of 1860. Headed for the silver mines in Arizona, Pumpelly said he looked forward to a pleasant trip until "the arrival of a woman and her brother dashed, at the very outset, my hopes of an easy journey."[3]

He had taken a seat in the rear of the coach. Its mounting on the thoroughbraces and heavy load in the boot caused the front end to tilt forward, making the rear seat the more desirable of the two. In a gentlemanly gesture, Pumpelly ceded this favored location to the woman. But soon, as he would admit, "I began to foresee the coming discomfort. The coach was fitted with three seats, and these were occupied by nine passengers. As the occupants of the front and middle seats faced each other, it was necessary for these six people to interlock their knees; and there being room inside for only ten of the twelve legs, each side of the coach was graced by a foot, now dangling near the wheel, now trying in vain to find a place of support. An unusually heavy mail in the boot, by weighing down the rear, kept those of us who were on the front seat constantly bent forward, thus, by taking away all support from our backs, rendering rest at all times out of the question."[4]

Technically, Butterfield's policy was that no more than four through seats be sold for one trip, which would not have made for any discomfort; but there seems to have been no limit set for way passengers, those riders picked up along the route.

William Tallack, a 29-year-old English Quaker, whose own eastbound journey in 1860 began with nine passengers and "an indefinite number" outside, added that ". . . an American vehicle is never 'full,' there being always room for 'one more'."[5]

The California Stage Company seemed to have taken the "always room for one more" policy to the extreme. The Sacramento *Union* twice within a few days recounted how a company stage overturned, one with 22 passengers on board, most of them on top, and the second with 23.[6]

A prominent San Francisco merchant found nothing amusing about his experiences and raked the company agents over the coals. He and three companions purchased their tickets for St. Louis in November of 1858 and were assured by the agent that they would be the only through passengers to the eastern terminus, through being the key word here.

Three way passengers accompanied them as far as Fort Yuma, a five to six day ride. They disembarked but two other passengers boarded at Tucson for El Paso. At that place, two others took their places for the remainder of the trip. Of his experience, the merchant wrote a lengthy jeremiad to the San Francisco *Bulletin*:

"The wagons of the Company can comfortably accommodate four passengers, and *no more*. All the space, exceeding forty-two inches (which is all that is allowed by the Company) that three grown men—suitably clad for night and day traveling in cold weather—require to be comfortable—just so much they will lack of being comfortable on an Overland mail wagon seat. Ordinary sized men have not the slightest chance of being at ease on their seats."[7]

The merchant thought the overcrowding during "incessant traveling night and day for so long a time . . . *mean treatment*," and wanted to warn passengers "to *know* before starting, what 'four through passengers' signifies; and then rely upon themselves for protection against these self-sufficient, autocratic way-agents."[8]

An anonymous correspondent, also writing to the San Francisco *Bulletin*, echoed much of the merchant's discord. "The greatest inconvenience we suffered during the journey was caused by the agents along the road crowding us with way-passengers. Certainly it was most unjustifiable, because they crowded in so many as to render all attempts at comfort or repose impossible."[9]

J. M. Farwell traveled overland in October of 1858 and experienced the same distress. "My notes along the road have been written under very embarrassing circumstances, six persons having been crowded into a coach intended for one-half the number, and the jolting and jamming being decidedly troublesome to either physical or mental exertion."[10]

The Butterfield company must have been elated by the events, however. So many people had requested seats from St. Louis to the west coast that lots were drawn to determine who went when. The story was the same on the other end. By the time the second eastern mail arrived in San Francisco, the Butterfield office there had more applications for through seats than could be accommodated.[11]

With a little foresight, Ormsby, the only through passenger on the historic maiden run west, would have counted his blessings. True, five other riders shared the Concord with him when it left Tipton, Missouri; but, one disembarked at the next station and the others, including John Butterfield, Sr., went only as far as Fort Smith, Arkansas, where the Concord was exchanged for a Celerity. After that, Ormsby mentioned no other riders until he reached Pilot Knob station in California, where an emigrant family of four boarded.

After three weeks alone with only the drivers and conductors to talk to, Ormsby seemed glad to share his space with the family and found the "joyous glee" of the eight-month-old baby "quite an addition to our company on the tedious road . . . ."[12]

Most other chroniclers, however, found families, and especially children, to be utter nuisances. Raphael Pumpelly, having foreseen his coming malaise, had very little regard for the family that travelled with him.

"My immediate neighbors were a tall Missourian, with his wife and two young daughters; and from this family arose a large part of the discomfort of the journey. The man was a border bully, armed with revolver, knife, and rifle; the woman, a very hag, ever following the disgusting habit of dipping—filling the air, and covering her clothes with snuff; the girls, for several days overcome by sea-sickness, and in this having no regard for the clothes of their neighbors;—these were circumstances which offered slight promise of comfort on a journey which, at the best, could only be tedious and difficult."[13]

Demas Barnes, who traveled over the Central Overland route in 1865, found his chivalrous nature stretched to the breaking point. "A through-ticket," he wrote "and fifteen inches of seat, with a fat man on one side, a poor widow on the other, a baby in your lap, a bandbox over your head, and three or four more persons immediately in front, leaning against your knees, makes the picture, as well as your sleeping place, for the trip . . . ."[14]

Barnes fancied himself a "friend of the ladies" and admitted he would endure discomforts himself at the expense of his gallantry; but, "I must say there are places where crinoline is out of order and babies become a downright nuisance!"[15]

At one stage of his journey he had as his traveling companions a "grass widow" and four children under the age of eight. "Each," he went on, "had a specific want at least once in twenty minutes, which divided by four, gave me a gentle hint exactly every five minutes . . . The first night—each one clambering for the soft place and crying over the accidental thumps, assisted by the gentle raps and kicks of the mother, who insisted upon their keeping perfectly still, and occasionally asking the gentleman [himself] if he would not reach the canteen or open the basket—was charming to a man who had six full days of sleep owing to him.

"The next day the children were covered with molasses and the stage with crumbs; and if you have never been here, I will inform you that dust, deep and thick, is the staple production of this country. Our condition is more easily imagined than described. When night came again I wrenched off the middle seat, piled in mail bags, blankets, and shawls, and spooned them in. They were so well tired out, I heard nothing of them until morning."[16]

Two Frenchmen, sharing a coach with four women between San Antonio and San Jose, had no children to contend with. At least, not at first. However, one of the women was very much along in a delicate condition and somewhere in California, decided this to be the time. A lady companion asked the driver to stop. Upon hearing the reason why, the driver promptly asked the men to leave the stage. They flatly refused, insisting that their fares did not call for them to be forced from the comfort of the coach. The hefty driver, a rugged frontiersman no doubt, persuaded them otherwise and told them to start walking; he would pick them up down the road. After the blessed event the vehicle continued its trip. Mother and baby were left at the first comfortable hotel where they were reported doing "prosperously."[17]

A twenty-five-year-old Mark Twain, on his way to Nevada with his brother Orion, over the Central Overland route in 1861, learned the hard way when to keep his own mouth shut. At first, the woman who boarded his coach ". . . was not a talkative woman," Twain wrote. "She would sit there in the gathering twilight and fasten her steadfast eyes on a mosquito rooting into her arm, and slowly she would raise her other hand till she had got his range, and then she would launch a slap at him that would have jolted a cow . . . she never missed her mosquito; she was a dead shot at short range."[18]

Twain, in his own inimitable manner, said he watched this "grim Sphinx" kill some thirty or forty of the insects and all the while "waited for her to say something, but she never did." Presently, he decided to open the conversation by remarking on the bad mosquito problem, to which she responded, "You bet!" and that was all it took. "Danged if I didn't begin to think you fellers was deef and dumb," she exclaimed, and afterwards subjected her fellow passengers to a "desolate deluge of trivial gossip."[19]

"How we suffered, suffered, suffered!" Twain wailed. "She went on, hour after hour, till I was sorry I ever opened the mosquito question . . . She never did stop again until she got to her journey's end toward daylight . . . ."[20]

Loss of sleep was the biggest complaint on crowded coaches. The Celerity, which Butterfield himself designed for travel over deserts, was used exclusively between Arkansas and eastern California. Lighter and less ornamented than the Concord, the Celerity was not only built for speed, but the middle seat was also hinged so that it could be lowered to make into a reasonably comfortable bed. However, it could work only if there were no more than two or three passengers.

Waterman Ormsby, in describing the manner in which the Celerity's seats folded down to make into a bed, added that when the stage is full, "the passengers must take turns at sleeping. Perhaps the jolting will be found disagreeable at first, but a few nights without sleeping will obviate that difficulty . . . ."[21]

William Tallack and his fellow passengers tried every manner of position to sleep and even cooperated so that some or all could rest. "Our sameness of posture becoming tedious, we tried various expedients by way of a change, sometimes slinging our feet by loops from the top of the waggon [sic], or letting them hang over the sides between the wheels, and at other times mutually accommodating each other by leaning or lying along the seats, and not seldom all nodding, for hours together in attitudes grotesque and diverse."[22]

For Raphael Pumpelly, days on the road without sleep were far more serious than mere discomfort and his experiences lean toward the macabre.

"The fatigue of uninterrupted travelling by day and night in a crowded coach," he wrote, "and in the most uncomfortable positions, was beginning to tell seriously upon all the passengers, and was producing a condition bordering on insanity. This was increased by the constant anxiety caused by the danger from Comanches. Every jolt of the stage, indeed any occurrence which started a passenger out of the state of drowsiness, was instantly magnified into an attack, and the nearest fellow-passenger was as likely to be taken for an Indian as for a friend. In some persons, this temporary mania developed itself to such a degree that their own safety and that of their fellow-travellers made it necessary to leave them at the nearest station, where sleep usually restored them before the arrival of the next stage . . . Instances have occurred of travellers jumping in this condition from the coach, and wandering off to a death from starvation upon the desert."[23] Frequent traveler Albert Richardson called it "stage-craziness."

Few descriptions were as poetic as that of Dr. Joseph C. Tucker, who had a "wild ride" over the Butterfield line in 1859.

"The wearied gunner," he wrote, "can sleep beneath his bellowing gun, the sailor amid the roar of ocean storm; but three on a seat in an open mud-wagon, tearing ten miles an hour through a wild country, is a situation calculated to set at defiance any such rest . . . the extended suffering was intense and poignant beyond description. You never encroached upon your neighbor, but upon waking you seldom failed to find him lying across you or snoring an apology into your ear. For we did sleep, somehow . . . . Often did I wake refreshed by a seeming sleep of hours . . . to be told by my watch that minutes only had elapsed. One poor fellow went crazy from loss of sleep; and to prevent mischief to himself and others, we were obliged to strap him fast in the boot, and leave him at the next station."[24]

Not everyone suffered from insomnia on the stagecoaches. H. D. Barrows and his bride spent their honeymoon in the winter of 1860-1861 on the Butterfield road. They had a hard time resting at first, ". . . but after a couple of days out, we could sleep without difficulty, either day or night."[25]

One may wonder why travelers didn't stop at one of the home stations and rest up a few days until the next coach going their way came along. Butterfield even provided for such eventualities; but he also had a warning to travelers contemplating doing so: "Passengers stopping from one stage to another, can only do so at their own risk as to the Company being able to carry them on a following stage."[26] It was a warning passengers did well to heed.

The Missouri *Republican* told of the woes of one passenger who had started for St. Louis a month earlier, stopped to rest for a few days at a station about halfway through the journey, and had since been unable to obtain a seat, all the coaches being full. He had even tried to bribe one driver with a bonus, to no avail.[27]

Every manner of personality and background rode the stagecoaches over the frontier and some of them would have given fiction writers enough material to fill volumes.

William Tallack, the prolific English traveler, wrote of a "long-bearded, shaggy-haired, rough-clad Texan" who boarded the stage at Visalia, California, bound for the Red River and who was simply called 'Texas.' Tallack seemed fascinated with the frontiersman, who had been to the gold fields in the Sierras and was now returning to his Texas home to get married. He kept Tallack enthralled with his tales of adventure and pioneering.

As the trip progressed, however, it was obvious that the tedium and difficulty in obtaining rest had begun to tell on Tallack's other companions, one of whom took advantage of a meal stop to move a mail bag which had been stowed between his seat and another. His action inconvenienced 'Texas' and the latter promptly moved the bag back to its original location. The first traveler motioned to the brace of pistols at his side and swore there would be trouble if the bags were moved again. This roused 'Texas' who put a hand on his own gun and growled, "Well, if you talk about 'trouble,' I can, too . . . . I'd as lief have 'trouble' as anything else." Intimidated by the frontiersman's stature, the other fellow settled back quietly for the remainder of the journey.[28]

A story from the most imaginative author could not have presented a more typically romantic western story than that which occurred on the overland stage carrying our good doctor, Joseph C. Tucker.

Just after crossing the Red River, probably at Sherman, Tucker reports that four passengers boarded, two men and two women, followed shortly thereafter by, in Tucker's words, ". . . a tall, handsome young fellow in boots and buckskins— bound for his ranch in Texas." It seems that everyone from that state was called 'Texas' and so was this fellow known in the exciting story that Tucker recounted.[29]

According to Tucker, the first four passengers kept to themselves and spoke only in French. He presumed that the younger man and woman, she a very attractive girl with "bright, black eyes," were more than just friends. He was overly attentive to her. Everything went well until the Texan boarded, then the girl became totally oblivious to the attentions of her companion and showed more than a casual interest in the tall, handsome stranger whose blonde hair fell in curls to his shoulders.[30]

At the next station, another passenger boarded, bringing the number to seven crammed into the Celerity. Tucker estimated their new companion's weight at 250 pounds. It was 'Texas' who called this new rider 'Dutchy.' When the latter insisted on sitting next to the door—a spot the Texan had enjoyed—'Texas' obliged and took up residence in the center of that same seat, probably the worst place on the coach.

It began to rain hard necessitating closing the window shades, which on the Celerity allowed for very little light or fresh air inside. Tucker and the Texan made do with the situation, passed around their flasks and told stories. The "Frenchys," as Tucker called them, remained apart and conversed only in their language, although the girl continued to throw a glance now and then at 'Texas.' Meanwhile, 'Dutchy' grew surlier for lack of fresh air.

"It was stifling," wrote Tucker. "We all wanted to smoke, but the presence of the women restrained us. Just then 'Dutchy' pulled an enormous pipe from his pocket, and, deliberately loading, proceeded to light and smoke it, despite the remonstrances of all." With the man blatantly ignoring one of the commandments for travelers, the women reacted as expected and the men cursed. But 'Dutchy' cared little for the comfort of his fellow riders and opened his window to a torrent of rain and wind. Just then, 'Texas' snatched the pipe from his companion's mouth and "flung it through the window."[31]

'Dutchy' wanted to fight, but he backed down when faced by the solidarity of the other men and settled back to drinking from his own supply. Soon, the alcohol lulled him to sleep, but even in slumber, his position as a *persona non grata* did not abate. Leaning against the door, 'Dutchy' began to snore loudly. With quiet approval from the others, 'Texas' reached behind him and turned the door latch so that it opened at the next good jolt. The fellow was sent flying out.

'Dutchy' was uninjured in the fall but so hopping mad, despite the Texan's overtures of aid, that he threatened everyone and was made to ride on the box. At the next station, he disembarked to get the law and the driver prudently went on without him.[32]

This was not the end of the trouble on this trip. It was, in fact, just the beginning. The young French girl's dark eyes had become more fixed upon the dashing frontiersman and the flourish with which 'Texas' accomplished his acts were no doubt intended to impress her. When the coach stopped for meals, he helped her down the steps; he brought her wildflowers; and at one point, he demonstrated his prowess with a pistol by dispatching a hawk in midair from the coach's window. When another hawk spooked and took to the air, 'Texas' gallantly offered his pistol to the lady with gestures that she try it.

Her young companion could take no more. Pushing the gun away, he exclaimed, in excellent English, "D - - n you, don't address this lady!" To which 'Texas' replied, "Well, Frenchy, you do speak English well enough to apologize at the next station."[33]

True to his nationality, the Frenchman took it as a challenge. The next station was a supper stop, just time enough to settle their differences. No white-gloved seconds counted off the paces here, nor was the ground of honor in some misty, early morning French wood. Instead, the showdown took place in the stage station's corral.

After some arguing over which weapons to use—the Frenchman wanted to use a pair of dueling pistols, the frontiersman, revolvers (the latter won)—shots were fired. The young Frenchman lay dead with a single shot through the heart.

The gunfire emptied the station but no one other than the dead man's companions paid much attention to the fallen duelist. After all, this was the wild West and one fallen gunfighter more or less did not justify delaying the mail a second longer than necessary. The coach made a hasty departure with only Tucker and the Texan aboard.

There had been much more to the foursome than either man had realized. According to the driver, the men were professional gamblers who had reputations of being "hard cases" along the border and were known to have killed many men. The older woman dealt faro for them and the girl was no doubt a new acquisition.[34]

Not all passengers traveling overland were so disposed to settle their arguments with gunplay, but one thing they all shared by journey's end was a general lack of cleanliness. Tallack took advantage of a brief stop at the Pecos River at three in the morning for "a hasty wash." He carried with him, "a sponge and towel, and several changes of linen . . . to be reached without trouble at a minute's notice, the time being very limited at the two or three opportunities of a bath which may occur during the journey. Many passengers go through the entire route without once changing their linen, and sometimes with the barest apology for washing."[35]

Phocion Way, an engraver from Ohio bound in 1858 for the Santa Rita mines in Arizona by way of the "Jackass Mail," entered this in his diary on May 30, eight days after leaving San Antonio:

"This is Sunday morning, but we will not even observe it so much as to put on a clean shirt. We all begin to present a rather wild appearance . . . . We have not changed our clothes since we started, nor shaved our faces (this makes no difference to me—I never shave) and the hot sun has made us almost as dark as the Indians."[36]

Personal hygiene, or the lack of it, on cross-country stagecoach travel would change very little over the decades. In 1876 the San Antonio *Daily Herald* printed this humorous piece:

"Not long ago one of our citizens, who never uses water as a beverage, and has not much use for it otherwise, left on the stage, for El Paso, some 700 miles. The day before he left a friend said to him: 'Bill, you had better buy a big canteen, fill it with cistern water, and take it along with you, as you will find good water scarce on the road.' The reply was: 'John, I guess I won't need it. I'll wash my face, anyhow, before I leave town.'"[37]

Most of the travelers over any long distance stage route often shared the wisdom of their experience with others who contemplated making the trip. One anonymous traveler over the Ox-Bow route in November of 1858 wrote: "Were I to travel the road over again, I would take but one pair of large, warm blankets, a revolver or shot-gun, and the stoutest suit of clothes I could get, with a strong, *loose* pair of boots, as several have had swelled feet . . . ."[38]

An article in a San Diego newspaper was even more specific in its recommendation to travelers over the San Antonio-San Diego route and suggested carrying the following:

"One Sharps rifle and a hundred cartridges; a Colt's navy revolver and two pounds of balls; a knife and sheath; a pair of thick boots and woolen pants; a half dozen pairs of thick woolen socks; six undershirts; three woolen overshirts; a wide-awake hat; a cheap sack coat; a soldier's overcoat; one pair of blankets in summer and two in winter; a piece of India rubber cloth for blankets; a pair of gauntlets; a small bag of needles, pins, a sponge, hair brush, comb, soap, etc., in an oil slick bag; two pairs of thick drawers, and three or four towels." All within easy reach![39]

Forget the fancy clad dandies and ladies who always step off a Hollywood stagecoach as fresh as when they first boarded. In no stretch of the imagination could a stagecoach traveler of the Southwest look like a fashion plate after a ride of a day or more. The window openings on western coaches did not have glass in them. And, with only fifteen inches allowed per body, bustles and hoop skirts were definitely out. Waterman Ormsby had a bit of sage advice: "White pants and kid gloves had better be discarded."[40]

Hats were another mode of fashion which were best left at home or packed away. An eastbound traveler in November of 1858 reported that all the men traveling with him lost their head "kivers" while sleeping. "Tie our hats on as we might, in the morning they were gone; and the owner might sigh in vain for another, for they were not obtainable until reaching El Paso or Fort Smith. There were twelve hats lost by us during the trip, which caused any amount of naughty words to be issued against the Company for placing six men in a stage only intended for four."[41]

Pumpelly also experienced the frustration of losing hats and estimated that some 1500 hats were probably lost each year by travelers, "for the benefit of the population along the road."[42]

At his own journey's end, Waterman Ormsby, when asked about the accommodations for passengers along the way, warned that they were not as comfortable as the Astor House in New York or their own homes and that "for much of the distance the traveller has to rough it in the roughest manner."[43]

Or, as Eli Perkins summed up his own trip, "It reminded me of a little jaunt I once took on a circular saw."[44]

Notes, Chapter Three

1. San Antonio *Herald*, 19 November 1858.
2. Omaha *Herald*, 1877.
3. Raphael Pumpelly, *Across America and Asia*, 1.
4. Ibid.
5. William Tallack, *The California Overland Express*, 23-24.
6. Sacramento *Union*, 19 October 1857. In Mae Helene Bacon Boggs, *My Playhouse Was A Concord Coach*, p. 287.
7. Walter Barnes Lang, *The First Overland Mail: Butterfield Trail, St. Louis to San Francisco, 1858-1861*, 85.
8. Ibid., 87.
9. Tallack, 73.
10. Lang, *The First Overland Mail, St. Louis to San Francisco*, 127.
11. New York *Herald*, 14 December 1858; Missouri *Republican*, 17 November 1858.
12. Waterman L. Ormsby, *The Butterfield Overland Mail*, 107-108.
13. Pumpelly, 1-2.
14. Demas Barnes, *From the Atlantic to the Pacific, Overland*, 8.
15. Ibid., 70.
16. Ibid., 70-71.
17. Sacramento *Union*, 11 May 1859. In Boggs, p. 338.
18. Mark Twain, *Roughing It*, 5.
19. Ibid., 6.
20. Ibid.
21. Ormsby, 94.
22. Tallack, 45.
23. Pumpelly, 4.
24. Dr. Joseph C. Tucker, *To the Golden Goal and Other Sketches*, 194-195.
25. Walter Barnes Lang, *The First Overland Mail: Butterfield Trail, San Francisco to Memphis, 1858-1861*, 65.
26. "Special Instructions to Conductors, Agents, Drivers & Employes" John Butterfield.
27. Missouri *Republican*, 13 December 1858.
28. Tallack, 29-30, 45-46.
29. Tucker, 182, 183.
30. Ibid., 183.
31. Ibid., 184-185.
32. Ibid., 185-186.

33. Ibid., 186-187.
34. Ibid., 187-193.
35. Tallack, 48.
36. William A. Duffen, Ed. "Overland Via 'Jackass Mail' in 1858, The Diary of Phocion R. Way" *Arizona and the West*, Vol. 2, No. 1, Spring 1960, 48.
37. San Antonio *Daily Herald*, 19 May 1876.
38. Lang, *The First Overland Mail, San Francisco to Memphis*, 43.
39. From the Hayes Collection, Bancroft Library, University of California, "Transcontinental Mails."
40. Ormsby, 94.
41. Lang, *The First Overland Mail, San Francisco to Memphis*, 42.
42. Pumpelly, 2.
43. Ormsby, 93.
44. San Antonio *Daily Herald*, 23 April 1875.

CHAPTER FOUR
"Every man must eat his peck of dirt"

*"The stomach . . . does not long remain
delicate after a few days of life on
the plains . . . ."[1]*

A correspondent who wrote for the San Francisco *Bulletin* under the pseudonym of "Occasional Correspondent," left the west coast on the Southern Overland in November of 1858 and said that he and his fellow travelers were "provided with ham, crackers, &c, which is a necessary precaution for passengers, as there is no place between Los Angeles and El Paso where a decent meal can be procured."[2]

"Occasional Correspondent" might have been misinformed; most accounts from eastbound travelers over the Ox-Bow route hinted that there wasn't a decent meal to be had until Missouri. Upon arriving in Los Angeles following his "wild ride" on the Overland in 1859, Joseph Tucker enjoyed his "first Christian meal since leaving Arkansas . . . ."[3]

Meals at the stations, particularly in those areas "west of civilization" on all of the overland routes, consisted mainly of hardtack, beans, jerky, and black coffee. Passengers who were accustomed to traveling by stage throughout the eastern half of the routes, then striking out for California by the same manner of conveyance would have experienced something of a shock to their culinary senses. Many of the meals at the stage stops in East Texas, for example,—usually inns or hotels— were not only palatable, but good. Some were downright exquisite. Not all, however, were either.

One French nobleman wrote cryptically in his diary of the food he found in an East Texas inn: "Fare distressingly bad, Crackers, potatoes (ind(igestible?) and Beef (tough), Coffee (very bad)."[4]

Frederick Law Olmsted experienced much the same during his journeys about Texas in the mid-1850s and reasoned that things would be different in Austin. "We had reckoned upon getting some change of diet when we reached the capital of the state . . . We reckoned without our host."[5]

Of breakfast he wrote: ". . . only the 'fry' had been changed for the worse before it was fried . . . Never did we see any wholesome food on that table. It was a succession of burnt flesh of swine and bulls, decaying vegetables [and] . . . rancid butter."[6]

Another traveler in East Texas described the facilities he found in a Marshall hotel as having a "pine knot bed with no 'kiver,' and a *well set* table with 'nothing to eat'."[7]

Some of the stagecoach inns, however, gained a reputation for not only setting good tables, but putting good food on them as well. A passenger on the Indianola-Seguin stage route enjoyed a "capital" breakfast at a Seguin station kept by J. R. Jefferson. It consisted of spareribs and back-bone, hominy, fresh eggs and milk, fried chicken, and "sweet, fresh bread."[8]

At Jane Long's Inn in Brazoria, travelers took pleasure in gourmet desserts with Madeira wine, and at the Excelsior House in Jefferson, such delicacies as orange-blossom muffins, purple plum nut bread, and Mayhaw jelly rounded out the menus.[9]

The Nimitz Hotel in Fredericksburg, northwest of San Antonio, was another favorite for travelers. "Mother" Nimitz' reputation for good German food, and especially her superb biscuits, spread up and down the stage lines. The Braches' Home in Gonzales fed its patrons home-grown vegetables, butter, eggs, meat, and milk.[10] Travelers could be particularly thankful for the milk as it was an unknown commodity at most stations.

But few could equal the fare found at the Camp Inn in Navasota, where travelers could expect to find fresh quail on the table one day, bear, turkey, or venison on another. In fact, quail were so numerous in the area that Ira Camp refused to serve chicken, thinking the dish too modest for his diners. Passengers on the coaches that stopped at the Old Moos Homestead in San Antonio were in for a special treat, for John Moos brewed his own beer and shared the fruits of his labors with his patrons.[11]

What had to be the most elegant of the stagecoach inn meals, however, were those served at the Menger Hotel in San Antonio where menus included wild turkey, buffalo tongue, venison, quail, turtle soup, and fresh fruits and vegetables, all washed down with the finest of wines. And, since William Menger raised his own hogs, fresh pork, bacon, ham, and sausage were also menu regulars.[12]

What a shock the stage passenger would find were he to journey from the civilized world of the Mengers and Camp Inns and their lavish repasts to the lonely stations on the overland routes. Such unpleasantries met Waterman Ormsby at Connolly's Station west of Gainesville in North Texas.

"The breakfast" he wrote, "was served on the bottom of a candle box, and such as sat down were perched on inverted pails or nature's chair. There were no plates and but four tin cups for the coffee, which was served without milk or sugar. As there were six of us, including drivers and workmen, those not lucky enough to get a first cup had to wait for the second table."[13]

According to Ormsby, however, there was barely time for a first table, let alone a second. ". . . we were advised by the host to 'hurry up before the chickens eat it'—which we did, to the no little discomfiture of the chickens." Despite the fact that the shortcake was the only edible portion of the meal, the breakfast tasted good to the New York reporter. "I can assure you that it would doubtless taste as well to any one coming over the same route . . . ."[14]

Ormsby probably looked back on this meal with great fondness the farther west he traveled. At Abercrombie Pass Station, in present Taylor County, Texas, he wrote that his "standard" breakfast was cooked by an old woman ". . . who, if cleanliness is next to godliness, would stand but little chance of heaven. There is an old saying that 'every man must eat his peck of dirt.' I think I have had good measure with my peck on this trip . . . ."[15]

Breakfast at Delaware Springs, just east of the Guadalupe Mountains, presented yet another novelty for Ormsby, jerky cooked over buffalo chips, which he was quick to define as making an excellent manure. Coffee was not to be had so Ormsby had to content himself with the jerky, ". . . raw onions, crackers slightly wormy, and a bit of bacon. The stomach, however, does not long remain delicate after a few days of life on the plains, and our breakfast was quite acceptable to me, notwithstanding the buffalo 'chips'. . . at first [a] distasteful idea."[16]

Sometimes the station keepers were to be commended for their efforts under the circumstances. Many hours ahead of schedule, Ormsby's coach was not expected when it rolled into the Head of Concho Station early on Saturday morning of September 25. The Butterfield employees may have even felt a moment of panic when they heard the coach horn signaling the approaching stage. The station was one of those which had not been completed when the first coach arrived; the men were living in tents and the corral was nothing more than a border of bushes. Still, Ormsby was impressed by their efficiency to get them on their way and considered the hurried breakfast of broiled bacon, shortcake, and coffee "quite an aristocratic meal for so early a settlement . . . ."[17]

One of the "Hints for Plains Travelers" advised, "Don't growl at food [served] at [the] stations . . . stage companies generally provide the best they can get."[18]

Still there were those times when only extreme hunger could induce a traveler to eat at one of these stations, such as Mark Twain's experience at an adobe station somewhere on the plains of the Central Overland. The table, although seemingly well set with a tin plate and cup, knife, and fork at each place, was nothing more than "a greasy board on stilts ... There was only one cruet left, and that was a stopperless, fly-specked, broken-necked thing, with two inches of vinegar in it, and a dozen preserved flies with their heels up and looking sorry they had invested there." The meal itself consisted of hard bread, bacon (which Twain was sure was condemned army issue), and "Slumgullion tea." The latter, Twain continued, had "too much dish-rag, and sand, and old bacon-rind in it to deceive the intelligent traveler."[19] No one ate the meal, which incidentally cost $1.00 each.

William Tallack had a similar experience at Fort Chadbourne. "Our table and food were black with clustering flies," he wrote, "which crowded even into our tea, and had to be spooned out by wholesale."[20]

But Tallack was more inclined to keep his culinary experiences on the Butterfield route in perspective. "Meals (at extra charge)," he wrote, "are provided for the passengers twice a day. The fare, though rough, is better than could be expected so far from civilized districts, and consists of bread, tea, and fried steaks of bacon, venison, antelope, or mule flesh—the latter tough enough. Milk, butter, and vegetables can only be met with towards the two ends of the route—that is, in California and at the 'stations' in the settled parts of the western Mississippi Valley."[21]

The Butterfield company itself more or less warned passengers what they could expect along the way:

> "The meals and provisions for passengers are at their own expense, over and above the regular fare. The Company intend[s], as soon as possible, to have suitable meals at proper places prepared for passengers at a moderate cost."[22]

Ormsby also tended to be less critical in view of the agrestic conditions which the first mail coach had to face. Nearing the end of his pioneer journey, Ormsby found at Alamo Mocho Station in California that a dollar charged for a meal of crackers, pork, and coffee, was reasonable enough even though most other station keepers charged but half that. At journey's end, he did not hesitate to advise travelers to take with them as much nonperishable food as possible since "there are few accommodations for eating, beyond what are afforded by the company stations to their own employees."[23]

Many travelers did carry their own provisions. One wrote that he took along some bread and two boiled hams which he supplemented at the stations with coffee. No mention as to what occurred first, spoiled hams or a spoiled appetite for them.[24]

Meals could come at any time of the day or night. A traveler might have supper, or breakfast—it was often difficult to tell one from another due to the sameness of the menu—at one or three in the morning and not have another meal stop until midafternoon. At a station about forty miles east of the Pecos River, Tallack described a meal of stewed dried apples, steaks, and hot coffee, "and never ate a breakfast with a keener relish."[25] Of course, the fact that it had been sixteen hours since he had last eaten could have made it all the more keen.

By 1860 an eastbound traveler over the Butterfield could expect to find the first vestiges of civilized meals and facilities before reaching the Red River.

"With the uninhabited solitudes of the desert and prairie," Tallack wrote of their reaching the Cross Timbers of North Texas, "we have also left behind us the rough and often villainous station-keepers and their coarse fare. The stations hereabouts and henceforward are kept by persons who generally have . . . a store or farm, and whose accommodation and manners are a decided improvement on what we have hitherto met with. To-day we had green Indian-corn served as a vegetable for dinner . . . . Further on our bill of fare included at times potatoes, salads, pies, and honeycomb . . . ."[26]

Further along the road, Tallack mentioned an additional benefit of civilization. At a station in the Arkansas Ozarks, the evening meal was not only a grand spread that included eggs, honey, potatoes, beans, steaks, and pastry, but was served with courtesy. ". . . the latter," he wrote, "we do not always receive in addition, when in the plains or elsewhere." Such tables must have seemed a world away from the breakfasts of "tough steaks at four A.M. in [the] dirty, dusty adobe" of the deserts.[27]

No doubt courtesy did exist in some of those lonely stations, at least to the degree found anywhere on the frontier. Many accounts reflect the attentiveness of the friendly station keepers and, where present, their wives. But there were grievances as well for the lack of *bon ton.* In particular, a New Yorker who traveled by the Overland during its infancy in 1858 is said to have encountered a meal at a Texas station that his eastern acclimatized taste buds simply could not stomach. After staring for a moment at the plate of stale sourdough biscuits and rancid bacon floating in its own grease, the New Yorker pushed it aside and glanced meekly at the station's cook who is said to have growled at the timid diner, "All right, dammit, help yourself to the mustard."[28]

With game so abundant in the vicinities of many stations it was reasonable that wild meat made up a great part of the menus when it could be had. A traveler over the upper San Antonio-El Paso Road in the spring of 1869 described a hot supper at the Head of Concho Station "embracing such viands as buffalo veal steaks and antelope pie."[29]

All in all, however, this same correspondent, who used the *nom de plume* "Wanderer" in his letters to the San Antonio *Express,* was far from happy with the meals he found en route. "I must say I did not become enthusiastic over the food, and account for its meanness only upon the principle that [Ben] Ficklin thinks a traveler needs plenty of sand in his gizzard in traveling through this country—Please add 25 per cent on your next bill for wear and tear of one set of digestive organs."[30]

Our honeymooners, the H. D. Barrows, were evidently delighted in their entire journey over the Butterfield line. Never was there a disparaging word about their trip, including meals. His recollection of a meal stop at the Fort Phantom Hill Station was typical. Here, they were "regaled with a grand supper of buffalo steak, venison, etc., and a rousing fire to warm us up for the night's travel, that made us remember the place as we would an oasis in the desert."[31]

For those other overland travelers who found their meal experiences less than civilized, they might have taken heart in knowing that 'whatsoever the station keeper disheth out, so will he taketh into his own belly.'

Notes, Chapter Four

1. Waterman L. Ormsby, *The Butterfield Overland Mail*, 72.
2. "Notes of Travel by the Overland Mail." In Walter Barnes Lang, *The First Overland Mail: Butterfield Trail. San Francisco to Memphis, 1858-1861*, 82.
3. Dr. Joseph C. Tucker, *To the Golden Goal and Other Sketches*, 198.
4. John Hunter Herndon, "Diary of a Young Man in Houston, 1838." In Muir, Andrew Forrest, Ed., *Southwestern Historical Quarterly*, Vol. LIII (1949-1950), 283.
5. Frederick Law Olmsted, *A Journey Through Texas, Or, a Saddle-Trip on the Southwestern Frontier*, 111.
6. Ibid., 112.
7. San Antonio *Herald*, 18 December 1857.
8. Ibid., 29 February 1860.
9. Kathryn Turner Carter, *Stagecoach Inns of Texas*, 4.
10. Ibid., 103, 114.
11. Ibid., 163, 194.
12. Ibid., 200-201.
13. Ormsby, 45.
14. Ibid.
15. Ibid., 51-52.
16. Ibid., 72.
17. Ibid., 63.
18. Omaha *Herald*, 1877.
19. Mark Twain, *Roughing It*, 17-18.
20. William Tallack, *The California Overland Express. The Longest Stage-Ride in the World*, 52.
21. Ibid., 23.
22. "Special Instructions to Conductors, Agents, Drivers & Employes," John Butterfield.
23. Ormsby, 93, 105.
24. Sherman *Democrat*, 3 August 1947.
25. Tallack, 50.
26. Ibid., 54.
27. Ibid., 36, 62.
28. W. Eugene Hollon, "Great Days of the Overland Stage," *American Heritage*, Vol. VIII, No. 4, 216. This same story, with slightly differing versions, was also told on the Central Overland Route and no doubt others as well.

29. San Antonio *Express,* 14 April 1869.
30. Ibid. Benjamin Franklin Ficklin was already experienced in the staging business when he took over the main line in Texas. Born in 1827 in Virginia, he began operating stage lines not long after serving a stint in the Mexican War. In 1859, he helped organize the Central Overland and Pikes Peak Express Company and helped in the organization and running of the Pony Express. After serving in the Confederacy, he received a government contract for a weekly mail service between Fort Smith, Arkansas and San Antonio with a branch line to El Paso, where he took over and rebuilt many of the abandoned Butterfield stations. He established his headquarters at the Concho Station, near the post of the same name. The community that grew up around the stage station became known as Ben Ficklin (also Benficklin) and enjoyed the status of being the county seat of Tom Green County until a flood in August of 1882 washed it away and the county seat was moved to San Angelo. Ben Ficklin died in Washington, D.C., in 1871 after choking on a fish bone.
31. H. D. Barrows, "A Two Thousand Mile Stage Ride." In Lang, 68.

CHAPTER FIVE
"We have . . . run a perfect gauntlet"

"You will be traveling through Indian
country and the safety of your person
cannot be vouchsafed by anyone but God."
(The Butterfield Overland Stage Co.)

God smiled upon the Butterfield Stage Company for "Admiral John's" swift-wagons were not attacked by hostiles until a westbound run in February of 1861 and that was the result of a general war, not an attack aimed at the line.

The same cannot be said, however, for the vehicles of other operators, especially those which journeyed over the long and perilous road between San Antonio, El Paso, and California.

A passenger just off the stagecoach from San Diego, California, in 1858, told a reporter of the San Antonio *Herald* that ". . . there is considerable apprehension felt from the Indians along the road to El Paso that the Indians seem more hostile, and are bolder than at any other time."[1]

In July of 1857, Edward Fitzgerald Beale, a few days out from San Antonio on his way to California with a caravan of government camels, was horrified at the evidence along the route. Almost daily it seems, his party came upon another mound of rocks marking some wayfarer's final resting place.

On July 7 he wrote, "We were passed on the road this morning by the monthly El Paso mail on its way up, by which I received, forwarded by some of my friends at San Antonio, a box of about two feet square, for which the moderate charge of twenty dollars was made. The dangers of this road, however, justified any price for such matters . . . in fact, from El Paso to San Antonio is but one long battle ground."[2]

Passengers who boarded the coaches on this route were wise to go loaded for bear and they usually did. "Everyone that leaves San Antonio for the West," wrote Phocian Way early in his journey in 1858, "goes well armed, and they do not conceal their arms but carry them in open view. When we entered the stage we found our two fellow passengers with their belts buckled around their waists with large Colt revolvers, and their rifles by their sides.

"All this was new to me and looked a little strange—it looked like we were indeed going through a country of savages and ruffians. However, to be in the fashion, I buckled on my army also."[3]

To the Native American, particularly the Comanche and Apache whose existence depended upon the horse, the coming of the stagecoach must have seemed like a blessing from the great spirit. For, where there were stagecoaches, there were stations, and where there were stations, there were horses. At least, there were supposed to be horses. Butterfield and the proprietors of the San Antonio mail line tried to eliminate that temptation by using mules exclusively throughout Indian country. It didn't stop the raids on the lonely outposts, however. Indians ate mules or traded them for horses and goods in Mexico.

In the year that Butterfield was putting his line into order, he had placed the Indian problem at the top of his priorities. To placate the natives along his route, he had cattle distributed down the line and made an effort to hire only men who were not inclined to shoot first and ask questions later. Among the instructions to those in his employ was this one regarding Indians:

"A good look-out should be kept for Indians. No intercourse should be had with them, but let them alone; by no means annoy or wrong them. At all times an efficient guard should be kept, and such guard should always be *ready* for any emergency."[4]

The policy worked, to a degree. The Indians respected Butterfield, called him the "Great Chief of the Swift Wagons" and, although they raided the stations, they left his coaches alone. Still, traveling over the Ox-Bow was not without its close calls.

Like the time a party of several hundred Comanches swooped down upon one of Butterfield's Celeritys and spent the next few hours examining it, from top to bottom, from the wheels to the mail bags, until finally, the "swift-wagon" was allowed to go on its way.[5]

A correspondent for the San Francisco *Bulletin* traveling eastbound over the southern route in November of 1858 wrote about a scary moment between Soldier's Farewell and Barney's stations in present Southwestern New Mexico. It was night so the campfires ahead on the trail could be seen for some distance by the men on the box. The passengers were awakened and issued rifles and cartridges.

"We passed within twenty feet of their watch-fires . . . " the correspondent wrote. "The road was heavy with sand, and the mules could not move out of a fast walk . . . Our situation was very unpleasant . . . we were beyond assistance or succor of any kind."[6]

The hundred or so braves stood as the coach went by. "We passed them in silence," the writer continued, "and they gave us defiant looks of cool indifference. We were not sorry when the mules were at last pressed into a trot, and the last glimmer of their watch-fires faded in the distance."[7]

Armed to the teeth as the coach's riders were, they were still greatly outnumbered by the Indians who could have taken them at will. It was a point not lost by the correspondent.

"The Apaches not attacking the stage," he continued, "when they had the passengers so absolutely in their power, seems to confirm the promise of Mangus, their chief, that the mules, stages, or stations of the Overland Mail Company should not in any way be molested by his nation. How long this state of things may last, it would be useless for me to conjecture; but, for the present, the incident related above may be taken as evincing a peaceful intent."[8]

In December of 1858 a Butterfield coach passed at night between two Comanche campfires near the Concho River Station. Since the coach had just come from the station at Mustang Ponds, which had recently been attacked, everyone on board was prepared for the worst. But the Indians' hands-off policy toward Chief Butterfield's swift-wagons held.[9]

Another California reporter who traveled east over the Butterfield road in the fall of 1858 did not report any close calls, but he had some strong advice for the line's operators and for anyone wanting to make the journey.

J. M. Farwell, of the *Daily Alta California*, spotted Apache campfires soon after his stagecoach left Hueco Tanks Station, east of El Paso. At Grape Creek, he was told by the station keeper that Indians had raided just the day before, making off with seven mules and a horse.[10]

Farwell was pleased with the journey overall, but tempered his enthusiasm with this warning:

"I can advise no one to come by this route, until these Indians . . . are cleared out. We have so far as I can see, and from what I learn on the road, run a perfect gauntlet."[11]

Another eastbound coach ran the gauntlet through Apache Pass the following January. The pass, which Waterman Ormsby had referred to as "Doubtful Pass . . . the most dangerous portion of the Apache country," was located in the southeastern corner of what is now just within the state line of Arizona. From here it was thirty-five miles east to Stein's Peak Station and forty miles west to the infamous Dragoon Springs Station.[12]

Although Ormsby's coach didn't have any trouble in the pass, the riders of an eastbound coach in January of 1859 had to stop long enough to clear some rocks from the road. The rocks could have fallen naturally, but the passengers who talked with reporters at St. Louis were positive they had been placed intentionally.[13]

It was in Apache Pass in February of 1861 where the only Butterfield coach ever attacked by hostiles ran its gauntlet. An uneasy alliance of sorts had been in effect ever since the overland began rolling. But because of circumstances beyond Mr. Butterfield's control, war had been declared upon all whites by the Chiricahua Apache chief, Cochise.[14]

The east- and westbound coaches had met about halfway between Dragoon Springs and Apache Pass stations on the night of February 6, 1861. Stopping, as was customary to exchange news, the driver of the eastbound learned from the other that the way ahead was fraught with danger. Dried grass had been deliberately stacked on the road, possibly to be fired, and worst of all, an emigrant train had been attacked with no sign of survivors.

The driver of the eastbound weighed the possibilities. Apache Pass would have to be negotiated in the dark, a dreaded prospect even in the best of times. But, he had nine passengers on board, including a Butterfield superintendent inspecting the line, and all were heavily armed, so he decided to go on ahead to Apache Pass Station.

Entering the pass, the mules were whipped to their fastest and the gap was traveled without incident; but upon descending the eastern grade, shots rang out from the dark and two mules went down in their traces. The driver was also hit but remained in the box. Under a covering fire, two of the passengers cut the dead mules out of the harness and the stage proceeded to the station where it stayed the night.[15]

The Butterfield company's stations did not enjoy the same truce as its coaches. News arriving with each mail in St. Louis indicated that a virtual war between the Comanches and the line's employees seemed to exist. Large numbers of mules were run off from the Fort Phantom Hill Station; eleven mules from Delaware Springs; the station at Soldier's Farewell burned; a raid on the San Elizario Station. Over the winter of 1858-1859, it was reported that the Butterfield company lost some 223 head of mules and horses in raids on the stations.

The Comanches even took a herd near Fort Belknap that was being distributed to the beleaguered stations.[16]

Raphael Pumpelly thought the portion through the Llano Estacado to be particularly vulnerable from attacks by Comanches.

"Here we were constantly exposed to the raids of this fierce tribe . . . We consequently approached the stockade station-houses with considerable anxiety, not knowing whether we should find either keepers or horses. Over this part of the road no lights [coach lanterns] were used at night, and we were here exposed to the additional danger of having our necks broken by being upset."[17]

The problems the company was having in keeping their stations stocked did not go unnoticed by the editorialists of the San Antonio *Herald*, a paper which had verbally assaulted the Butterfield contract from the beginning. The *Herald* reported the news from a newly arrived passenger, one H. W. Allen, that eight mules and a horse had been taken in a raid on Butterfield's Cottonwood Springs Station in Limpia Canyon. A few months earlier, the same paper had extolled the "safety" of their route to El Paso.[18]

But the San Antonio road was not a safe one. It was, as Edward Fitzgerald Beale said, one of the bloodiest stretches of stage road in the country. During the 31 years of the line chronicled by Wayne Austerman, between 1850 and 1881, no fewer than 47 attacks on coaches occurred (including holdups by highwaymen), with 12 coaches destroyed and many drivers and passengers killed. Some 103 stations were raided, many of them repeatedly, with 20 instances of stations being destroyed.[19]

Some of the descriptions of attacks were nothing short of spectacular. In May of 1861 an incident occurred near Fort Davis that would have done any Hollywood director proud.

Driver Parker Burnham and Jim Spears were on the box when their coach was attacked by Mescalero Apaches three miles from Barrilla Springs. The mules were urged to their utmost while arrows flew at the coach like a horde of locusts at a grain field. Burnham was hit twice and slumped into the boot as Spears took the reins. Some of the mules were running with shafts imbedded in their sides and barely outran the Indians to the station. Just as the coach passed through the gate into the corral, one of the animals dropped dead. Burnham recovered but decided this was much too dangerous and joined the Confederate army.[20]

Burnham wasn't the only driver to tire of tempting fate. After his San Antonio-El Paso coach barely avoided an attack on Fort Lancaster and an ambush further on, William Hobson also made up his mind to do something else for a living. "I intend to quit this line after this trip," he told a *Herald* reporter, "as this is the second time I have missed by a scratch. The pay is not enough for the risk, so look for me in San Antonio next month, if I make the trip safe."[21]

The perils still existed on the route in the 1870s, according to Texas Ranger James Gillett. "El Paso was seven hundred and fifty miles by stage from San Antonio or Austin and the journey required about seven days and nights of travel over a dangerous route—an unusually hard trip for any passenger attempting it."[22]

Limpia Canyon in the Apache [Davis] Mountains was one of the most dangerous portions of the overland routes in Texas. The narrow defile, described by Nathanial Taylor as being fifty feet at its narrowest and five hundred at the widest, winds for some fifteen miles between towering basaltic cliffs. Taylor thought it was a perfect place for Indian attacks and expressed his apprehension to the driver.

"This is certainly a dangerous place," Taylor said. "If one should be attacked here, what possible chance of escape?" To which the driver replied: "It is the safest place this side of San Antonio. No Indians were ever known to enter this canyon. They want a chance to retreat and slip out . . . you'll never catch them coming into this trap."[23]

The driver was either ignorant or being reassuring for his passenger. Attacks on mail coaches and caravans were quite regular within Limpia Canyon and vicinity. One particular attack was not without its lighter moment.

In 1859 Apaches set upon a stagecoach of the San Antonio-El Paso company in Limpia Canyon, killed the driver, and made off with the mail bags. Upon reaching their secluded camp, the Indians began going through the bags' contents which included several issues of *Harper's Weekly* and *Frank Leslie's Illustrated Newspaper*. Having never seen pictures on paper, they became so engrossed that they were caught completely off guard by a patrol from Fort Davis. Most of the Indians were killed, but those who escaped spread the word that the strange pictures had revealed their location and were bad medicine.

If awards could be handed out to drivers for their skill under fire, most votes would certainly have to go to one Henry W. Daly.

Daly drove for the Ben Ficklin line after the Civil War. The postwar road from San Antonio west branched at Fort Concho, one fork leading northeast to Jacksboro, the other southwest to El Paso. After driving for a year on the Jacksboro road, a "fairly quiet" one, Daly was transferred to the El Paso branch, where a "cavalryman rode on the seat with each driver and rifles were distributed among the passengers."[24]

One day near the Flat Rocks on the Staked Plains, Daly's coach was ambushed by Comanches. When the Indians opened fire, a shot severed the reins and Daly had no control whatever over the mules, which were, by now, running full bore. Daly could tell the Indians were after the animals because they concentrated their fire at the coach hoping to disable it rather than shooting the mules. "The next station," he wrote, "Melborne Crossing on the Pecos, was a long run, and from the way one of the front wheels was wobbling I feared we would not make it."[25]

Two of the braves drew within fifty yards of the coach; the cavalryman on the box hit one of them and a passenger shot the other's horse out from under him. By now, all four mules were covered with lather and one was bleeding profusely. "But we were nearing the station," Daly recalled. "Once again two Indians bore in on us. When our riflemen dismounted them the party gave up the chase." The mules, doing what stagecoach mules did best, ran without guidance or control to the station.[26]

That incident alone would have been more than enough to last any man an entire career. But Daly had yet another, even more hair-raising experience.

"From a driving standpoint," he wrote, "the most dangerous piece of road east of the Pecos [River] was over Lancaster Hill ... Near the crest the road entered a defile of rock so narrow that two teams could hardly pass. Then came a long steep incline cut in the hillside, after which the road, following the contour of the mountain, turned left at almost a forty-five degree angle. This point was always a source of anxiety because the rains cut great ruts across the roadway. It was best to take this turn at a walk because the lead mules would virtually be out of sight before the coach started to change direction. Shortly beyond this was a right-hand turn ... then another long incline with the hillside on one hand and space on the other. Snuggled at the bottom was Lancaster station and an abandoned army post."[27]

In 1867 Daly's coach was attacked just as it neared the summit where Indians began jumping down from the cliffs. They tried to grab the mules' bridles, but Daly lashed at them with his whip and sent the team through the gap at a run. He described the air as black with arrows while Jim Spears directed the passengers' fire from inside the coach.

The coach all but flew down Lancaster Hill. "As we thundered toward the turn," Daly wrote, "I believed my last moment had come, and I may say that that is the only time I have ever had that feeling."[28]

One Indian jumped down upon the rushing team and reached for the bridle of one of the lead mules. Daly hit him squarely in the face with his whip and sent him flying. "The next I knew the mules were careening around the turn. The wheels left the ground and the whole coach seemed to swing out over space. I could see the harness tighten and strain. Then we hit, on two wheels, careening so that I had to grasp the seat. It required some seconds for me to realize that we were actually on the road, and to this day I don't see how we got there."[29]

The Indians kept up their attack until guards from the station could be seen coming to the aid of the stagecoach. Only when the vehicle was safe in the station yard did it become clear just how miraculous their deliverance had been. Two passengers were wounded and Daly himself had two arrows in his back. "The coach and mules were so full of arrows," he wrote, "that they resembled pin cushions." When Jim Spears asked him how he managed that turn, Daly, a true reinsman if there ever was one, replied, "the mules managed it."[30]

In May of 1863 a stagecoach was attacked near Deep Creek Station in far western Utah. One of the wheel horses was shot and killed. Driver Nick Wilson described his ordeal:

"I threw off the brake, cracked my whip and away we went, plunging down the hill and dragging the dead horse along until we were out of gunshot range. I stopped the team and unharnessed the dead horse, hitched one of my leaders in its place and made it into Deep Creek Station."[31]

"Downing the Nigh Leader," by Frederic Remington. The quickest, most efficient method to stop a stagecoach was to disable one of the horses or mules in the team, particularly one of the leaders. (Courtesy Denver Public Library, Western History Department)

Most drivers were loyal to their profession and many gave their lives in an effort to protect the passengers and the mail. Every now and then, there was an exception. In one such incident on the Central Overland route, the driver declared ahead of time that it was every man for himself in the case of an attack. He said he would take a lead horse and skedaddle. However, two of the male passengers were well armed and they convinced him otherwise.

Some of the incidents involving Indians had their humorous overtones. Comanches that raided a Butterfield station for mules between Fort Chadbourne and El Paso seemed almost apologetic and told the station keeper that if he ever needed the livestock more than they, he could come and get them back. It is highly unlikely that he did.[32]

Early in 1870 August Santleben, who owned and drove coaches between San Antonio and Mexico, rode as a passenger westward from old Bexar to Fort Stockton. Besides Santleben, there were two other men in the well-guarded coach. A nun, Sister St. Stephen, boarded at Fort Concho. With the military escort and the armed male passengers, no one felt uneasy over Indians. Santleben described the nun as an "entertaining traveling companion," who took the men's good-natured humor in stride. "Once I ventured to say that she could be of no service in case we were attacked by Indians. She laughed and replied that if such an event should happen, her part would be attended to equally as well as ours; that we should do the fighting and she would do the praying."[33]

The Indian threat was just as bad, if not worse, on the northern routes, especially during the Plains Indian Wars of the 1860s and '70s when the Native Americans viewed the increased incursions as a threat to their way of life. The problem got so bad in Utah that it took one load of mail four months to reach Salt Lake City from Atchison, Kansas. During one month in 1864, only one coach made it through to Salt Lake from the east.

The stations were raided with such frequency that more than two dozen were abandoned at one point. By summer of 1862 every station from the Platte River to Fort Bridger had been hit and burned. Finally, no fewer than two stagecoaches were ordered to travel together west of Julesburg, Colorado.

Indians weren't the only menace on the stage roads by any means. Highwaymen found the vehicles and their passengers easy prey and prime pickings. Again, John Butterfield looked ahead to all possibilities and instructed that no "money, jewelry, bank notes, or valuables of any nature, will be allowed to be carried under any circumstances whatever."[34]

But other lines, both short- and long-distance stages, suffered greatly from holdups. Most road heists occurred after the Civil War when it seemed that every hooligan on the run picked Texas to hide in. Not all the bandits, however, fit the stereotype of the ordinary highwayman.

Santleben described the Mexican bandits, or *ladrones*, as being well dressed and equally mounted, with both theirs and their horses' attire liberally ornamented with silver. Although heavily armed, they were always polite in their demands for the passengers' valuables. Santleben had only one close call from the *ladrones*, but he had his share of other near misses, including one in 1867 on a return trip from Eagle Pass.

At Castroville, some 25 miles west of San Antonio, he had just received the mail sack for San Antonio and handed the postmaster a $20 gold piece from a bag containing about $50 in Mexican silver. The transaction did not go unnoticed by two men loitering nearby who immediately purchased two seats on the coach. Santleben was not suspicious of the pair at first and was glad to have the company, there being no other riders.

During the four miles to his father's house, where the team was changed, Santleben began to feel uneasy about his two passengers. While the fresh team was being harnessed, he greased the axles of the wagon then returned the four-pound monkey wrench to its place in the toolbox kept up front. "When ready to start," he wrote, "I noticed that the cushion of the rear seat, which my passengers were waiting to occupy, did not fit properly, and I reached over to straighten it. As I raised the right-hand end I saw under it the monkey wrench that I had replaced in its proper receptacle a half-hour before." Santleben confronted them with their "murderous intentions" and sent them packing. He later learned that they were deserters from the army.[35]

Like their Indian counterparts, highwaymen liked to choose places along the road where the stagecoach was the most vulnerable, such as Pegleg Crossing on the San Saba River between Forts Mason and McKavett.

Approaching Pegleg Station from the southeast, the road followed a wide valley between some hills. Outbound from the station, the road descended a steep hill to the crossing on McDougal Creek. Here, the driver had to brake hard to keep his vehicle from winding up as cordwood at the bottom. After fording the creek, the road followed the south bank of the San Saba to just above Ten-Mile Crossing where it crossed the river. Before the crossing, however, the trail came to the most dreaded portion of the route, a steep ascent up the west bank through a draw. Overlooking the draw was a prominent hill which became known as Robbers' Roost.

The names Dick Dublin and Pegleg Crossing became synonymous, his gang literally held the place hostage. Texas Rangers accompanied the coach for a while, but, of course, it was never stopped when they were on board. When at last, in 1878, the rangers captured Bill Allison, one of Dublin's men, and his compadres failed to spring him, Bill talked and the flagrant robberies at Pegleg Crossing came to an end.[36]

Between 1876 and 1883, as the Indian threat lessened, highwaymen grew bolder and stagecoach holdups increased across the Texas frontier. Coaches were stopped with impunity on the banks of the Clear Fork of the Trinity, just a mile from the Fort Worth post office. These daring robberies were finally ended when lawmen, camped hidden in the trees near the river and armed with long range rifles, pursued an effective policy of shooting first and asking questions later. Veteran driver Joe Hunter, however, said that his job became monotonous after the holdups ended.[37]

Drivers no doubt had orders never to put the passengers at risk when looking down the barrel of a highwayman's gun. Alone, they could do as they dared. When one driver on the U.S. Stage Line from San Antonio to Alleytown was stopped ten miles west of Columbus and refused to give the robbers the mail bags, they coldly shot the coach horses down, then made no further attempt to take the bags.[38]

These so-called 'Knights of the Road' weren't particular who they robbed and they certainly weren't impressed by army brass. In 1872 the stagecoach running between San Angelo and San Antonio was stopped. All of the passengers were army officers, including a lieutenant colonel, and all contributed to the welfare of the thieves without resistance. When the incident was told to their fellow officers at Fort Concho, one "fine looking officer from New York," who had nothing but contempt for highwaymen, bragged about what he would do if they ever attempted to rob him. Sure enough, the next time he journeyed to San Antonio, his coach was stopped and his bravado went the way of the others.[39]

When the westbound coach on the road between San Angelo and Ballinger was waylaid on the night of October 15, 1887, the thieves had already stopped the eastbound, realizing some $1,300 from its eleven passengers, and were calmly holding it hostage while awaiting the arrival of the other. W. J. Ellis, who was driving the westbound, said that there were two preachers among his nine passengers, one of which grew overly bold. Directing his attention to one of the thieves, the preacher bellowed, "Sir, I believe I know you and I think you have heard me preach." The culprit being addressed took no heed, rounded up $450 from the victims, then bid "us to be good and loped off."[40]

A year later Ellis' coach was halted again on the same road and the lone robber took all the cash and valuables from the fourteen passengers despite their pleas that their treasures had only personal value. The bandit went on about his nasty chore while snorting that they were the most sentimental bunch of people he had ever robbed.[41]

Just as the Dublin gang had controlled Pegleg Crossing, so did bandits dominate the road between San Angelo and Abilene, Texas, where two men named Potter and McDonald ambushed stagecoaches seven times within a three-month period over the winter of 1884. W. J. Ellis recalled how the

☞Agents of W., F. & Co. will <u>not</u> post this circular, but place them in the hands of your local and county officers, and reliable citizens in your region. Officers and citizens receiving them are respectfully requested to preserve them for future reference.

Agents WILL PRESERVE a copy on file in their office.

$800.00 Reward!

ARREST STAGE ROBBER !

1.

On the 3d of August, 1877, the stage from Fort Ross to Russian River was stopped by one man, who took from the Express box about $300, coin, and a check for $305.52, on Grangers' Bank of San Francisco, in favor of Fisk Bros. The Mail was also robbed. On one of the Way Bills left with the box the Robber wrote as follows:—

"I've labored long and hard for bread—
For honor and for riches—
But on my corns too long you've trod,
You fine haired sons of bitches.
BLACK BART, the P o 8.

Driver, give my respects to our friend, the other driver; but I really had a notion to hang my old disguise hat on his weather eye." (*fac simile.*)

Respectfully

B. B

It is believed that he went to the Town of Guerneville about daylight next morning.

2.

About one year after above robbery, July 25th, 1878, the Stage from Quincy to Oroville was stopped by one man, and W., F. & Co's box robbed of $379, coin, one Diamond Ring, (said to be worth $200) one Silver Watch, valued at $25. The Mail was also robbed. In the box, when found next day, was the following, (*fac simile*):—

*here I lay me down to sleep
to wait the coming morrow
perhaps success perhaps defeat
And everlasting sorrow
I've labored long and hard for bread
for honor and for riches
But on my corns too long you've trod
You fine haired sons of bitches
let come what will I'll try it on
My condition can't be worse
and if there's money in that Box
Tis munny in my purse*

*Black Bart
the Po8*

A reward poster for the infamous lone bandit, Black Bart, who was actually a very natty, benign looking gentleman named Charles Boles, who lived in San Francisco between his making life miserable for Wells Fargo. In his 28 or 29 holdups of the company coaches from 1875 to 1883, he took a total of only $18,000 in gold and never hurt anyone. His trademark was a poem left in the empty strongboxes such as this one and signed, "the po8," the poet. (Courtesy of Wells Fargo Bank) stagecoach would leave San Angelo at 4:00 A.M. and the robbers would invariably stop it six miles out of town.[42]

The boldness of some highwaymen bordered on the ludicrous.

"On one occasion after robbing the eastbound stage," according to Ellis, "when the westbound coach was delayed from Abilene on account of the heavy roads, they told the driver of the eastbound stage to tell the other driver to hurry up, as they were waiting for him and it was cold. The drivers met about thirty minutes later and the message was delivered."[43]

The humor of the incident turned sour, however, on the arrival of the westbound coach. Among the passengers were two lawmen, a U.S. Marshall, and a deputy. When the peace officers pulled their guns, the thieves opened fire, hitting the deputy in the breast. Spooked by the shots, the coach horses bolted and the robbers fired after the fleeing stage. One bullet passed through a trunk in the rear boot and lodged in the marshall's back. He was lucky, the bullet having spent most of its energy going through the trunk; but the deputy's wound proved fatal.[44]

The award for the nerviest bandit would have to go to the lone highwayman who stopped a stagecoach near San Angelo in April of 1888. He made the passengers get out and put sacks, which he provided, over their heads. After relieving them of their cash and valuables, he continued to hold them while waiting for the stage from the opposite direction.

During the four hours they were delayed, the passengers were entertained by the robber with stories of adventure and daring. He then wrote out a certificate for each passenger, citing their bravery and verifying that they had been robbed once. Finally, when the other stage failed to show, he bid all a pleasant journey and sent them on their way.[45]

After being relieved of their money and baggage, passengers on board a coach between Waco and Dawson, Texas, in 1860 would not have had the price for even a cup of coffee at the next stop had it not been for the ingenuity of one of their number. The coins that the elderly woman had carefully platted in her long hair were overlooked by the robbers and later shared with her fellow travelers.[46]

An Episcopal priest, the only passenger on a coach that was held up between San Antonio and San Marcos, learned that his calling had some unexpected benefits. When ordered to hand over his watch, the bishop said it was old and of no value to anyone but himself. "Also, I have very little money," he pleaded, "barely enough to carry me through this trip. You see a preacher is always a poor man." When the thief learned that the man of the cloth was Episcopalian, he apologized heartily. "Hell! That's my own church," he bellowed and sent the bishop on his way still in possession of his money and his watch.[47]

As the coach pulled away, the bishop might have recalled an old Latin saying: *'Vacuus cantat coram latrone viator'*; 'The traveler with an empty purse sings in presence of the highwayman.'

The number of stage holdups decreased after 1883, what with improved law enforcement and fewer stages to rob. Train robberies increased, however, as tracks replaced the stage roads, a point old-timers and staging devotees found amusing. In 1916 possibly the last stagecoach holdup in the United States in which a driver was killed occurred near Jarbridge, Nevada. The coach was found by a search party when it didn't arrive on its regular run from Rogerson, its driver brutally murdered, and $4,000 missing from the mail bags. Like countless other robberies, the loot was never recovered, the highwaymen usually going to their graves with the secrets of the treasures' whereabouts.[48]

In Texas, the Mason *News* in September of 1888 commented upon the last of the stagecoach robbers in that part of the country: "San Angelo is now a railroad point, and the lone highwayman has gone to California, seeking better fields."[49]

Notes, Chapter Five

1. San Antonio *Herald*, 20 April 1858.
2. Lewis Burt Lesley, *Uncle Sam's Camels*, 152-155.
3. William A. Duffen, Ed., "Overland Via 'Jackass Mail' in 1858. The Diary of Phocion R. Way," *Arizona and the West*, 42.
4. "Special Instructions to Conductors, Agents, Drivers & Employes." John Butterfield.
5. Capt. William Banning and George Hugh Banning, *Six Horses*, 147.
6. Walter Barnes Lang, *The First Overland Mail: Butterfield Trail. San Francisco to Memphis, 1858-1861*, 33.
7. Ibid.
8. Ibid. Mangas Coloradas was the chief of the Mimbres Apaches.
9. Missouri *Republican*, 3 and 5 January 1859.
10. Lang, *The First Overland Mail . . . St. Louis to San Francisco. 1858-1861*, 121, 124.
11. Ibid., 124.
12. Waterman L. Ormsby, *The Butterfield Overland Mail*, 83-84. On the night of 8 September 1858, tragedy struck Dragoon Springs, one of the Butterfield stations. The station was in the process of being completed when the three Mexican laborers inexplicably turned on the four company employees in the middle of the night. The only survivor among the latter was Silas St. John. Grievously wounded with a near severed arm, he lay alone with his dead and dying companions for four days before help arrived.
13. Missouri *Republican*, 4 February 1859.
14. Cochise had been trading peacefully with Apache Pass Station and even had a contract with the mail company to cut firewood for the stage stand. But, in February of 1861 a Lieutenant George Bascom mistakenly linked Cochise's band with the recent kidnapping of a Mexican boy. On the pretense of a parley, Bascom lured Cochise into a trap. The chief escaped but five members of his family did not. Cochise then captured an employee of the mail station and two men from an emigrant train and suggested an exchange. Bascom refused, Cochise killed his captives, and Bascom retaliated by hanging three of Cochise's family. In the all-out war that followed, the Apaches destroyed eight stations between Cooke's Spring and Tucson;

six coaches were burned, and thirty men killed, including George Giddings' brother James.

15. An attack was made on the station the next day during which the agent, C. W. Culver, was wounded, an employee killed, and another captured by the Apaches.
16. Ibid., 1, 7, and 10 February, 3, 7, 10, and 14 March 1859.
17. Raphael Pumpelly, *Across America and Asia*, 3-4.
18. San Antonio *Herald*, 1 July 1859, and 1 December 1859.
19. Wayne R. Austerman, *Sharps Rifles and Spanish Mules*, 315-323. Douglas McChristian, "Incidents Involving Hostile Indians Within the Influence of Fort Davis, Texas, 1866-1891," lists 13 attacks on stagecoaches or stations within the environs of Fort Davis alone between January 1869, and January of 1881.
20. Emmie Giddings W. Mahon and Chester V. Kielman, "George Giddings and the San Antonio-San Diego Mail Line," 232; San Antonio *Daily Express*, 1 June 1902.
21. San Antonio *Herald*, 8 January 1868.
22. James B. Gillett, *Six Years With the Texas Rangers. 1875 to 1881*, 137.
23. Col. Nathaniel Alston Taylor, *The Coming Empire, or, Two Thousand Miles in Texas on Horseback*, 356.
24. Henry W. Daly, "A Dangerous Dash Down Lancaster Hill," *Frontier Times*, 171.
25. Ibid.
26. Ibid., 172.
27. Ibid. The abandoned post was Fort Lancaster. Today, a state highway still descends Lancaster Hill and the fort's ruins are a State Historic Park.
28. Ibid., 172-173.
29. Ibid., 173.
30. Ibid.
31. George A. Thompson, *Throw Down the Box!*, 27.
32. Banning, 149.
33. August Santleben, *A Texas Pioneer. Early Staging and Overland Freighting Days on the Frontier of Texas and Mexico*, 121-122.
34. "Special Instructions."
35. Santleben, 54.
36. Robert S. Weddle, "The Pegleg Stage Robbers," *Southwest Heritage*, 2-5.
37. Capt. B. B. Paddock, Ed., *History of Texas: Fort Worth and the Texas Northwest Edition*, 876.
38. San Antonio *Herald*, 19 January 1868.

39. J. D. Fauntleroy, "Old Stage Routes of Texas," *Frontier Times*, 423.
40. "Tells of Depredations of Early Day Robber," *Frontier Times*, 423.
41. Ibid.
42. "Depredations," 424.
43. Ibid.
44. Ibid.
45. W. C. Holden, "Law and Lawlessness on the Texas Frontier, 1875-1890." *The Southwestern Historical Quarterly*, 195-196.
46. Alva Taylor, "Taylor's History and Photographs of Corsicana and Navarro County," 41. In Kathryn Carter, *Stagecoach Inns of Texas*, 97.
47. "Depredations," 423.
48. Thompson, 137. Thompson detailed one famous company's loss due to highwaymen. During the period from 1870-1884, Wells Fargo suffered a loss of $928,000, with $415,000 of that amount coming from the robberies alone. Most of the rest of the amount was paid in guards' salaries. During that same period, Wells Fargo numbered 313 stagecoaches robbed, with five drivers and guards killed and four fatalities among the passengers. But, 23 doers of the deeds had their comeuppance, almost half killed while resisting arrest. Thompson remarks that these numbers were most likely far too conservative. As often as not, if the thief was caught by a citizen's posse, his arraignment, trial, sentencing, and burial were carried out on the spot.
49. Holden, 196.

CHAPTER SIX
" ... nothing is wanting to insure safety"

"I shall be glad to furnish Mail Escorts, as long as they are wanted, but they must be properly treated."[1]

So where was the United States Cavalry during these attacks on mail coaches and stations? Why didn't they come charging over the hill to the rescue with bugles blaring?

It did happen on occasion; but, more often than not, the army's role in protecting the mail and passengers was no more dramatic than a small mounted escort or a lone trooper "riding shotgun" on the box. It wasn't a matter of not caring on the part of the military, but one of logistics and sheer mathematics. The forts were simply too far apart and usually undermanned.

Late in 1857 the Secretary of War issued orders to the commanding officers of all the posts between San Antonio and San Diego to furnish escorts of at least fifteen men to every coach when required. The following year General David E. Twiggs, commander of the army in Texas, admitted there was a need for more military protection, but declared ". . . *I have not the force to do it.*"[2]

By then, there were only seven forts to guard some seven hundred miles between San Antonio and El Paso, and many of the garrisons were infantry. Even fewer garrisons protected the early Butterfield route. In fact, there was not another post on the overland road between Forts Chadbourne and Bliss, a distance of more than four hundred miles.

Passengers who arrived in St. Louis with the tenth mail on November 14, 1858, reported seeing large numbers of Indians, although there was never any show of hostility. Still, the Missouri *Republican* blasted the government for what seemed a total indifference to protect the mail line: "It is very certain that the overland mail has proved itself worthy of all the protection and support that can be given it . . . ."[3]

Waterman Ormsby also saw that the road needed more military protection and suggested that soldiers be distributed along the route instead of congregated in populated areas. To do otherwise, he said, was "trifling with human life."[4]

As a matter of record, no additional posts were ever established on that 400-mile stretch while the Butterfield line was in operation on the Ox-Bow. Only when uncertain water supplies between Horsehead Crossing and El Paso, by way of the Guadalupe Mountains, forced the company to shift to a more southerly route, did the Butterfield stages enjoy the security of three additional forts, Stockton, Davis, and Quitman.

In reality, the safe delivery of the mail was as much in the army's interest as anyone's. The soldier looked forward to the sound of the coach horn, hoping for a letter from home. When a disabling epidemic hit the stage company's mule and horse populations in 1873, a disgruntled resident of Fort Concho wrote:

"We have been without mail during the last three or four weeks and but little hope is entertained of getting in possession of it for some time to come; all the animals of the different stage routes are . . . unable to travel . . . This is rather disagreeable to everybody as the arrival of the United States Mail forms a part of the little excitement on this isolated post and the mail is always eagerly expected."[5]

Mail escorts were not always trustworthy, as seen in a letter from the commanding officer at Fort Davis to his counterpart at Fort Clark. In the April 5, 1856, correspondence, Colonel Washington Seawell expressed his consternation over the conduct of some of his men on escort duty at the distant post.

"It is to be regretted, indeed, that the men in our service are of such bad characters as not always to enable us to select trust worthy or reliable men for an important service . . . .

"The desertion of the Corporal in Command, and the usual bad conduct of the mail escort generally, proves this, I think . . . ."[6]

The Civil War was the one of the major causes of the increased Indian problems of the post-1860s. Gains made in reducing the threat in the 1850s came unraveled when the United States was forced to evacuate the federal forts in 1861. Texans made an effort to man them, but were too short-handed and ill supplied to make a difference so that they, too, were forced to abandon the posts. A vacuum was created and the Indians filled it.

A returning federal army in 1865 and 1866 found the Indian situation worse than before the war. In October of 1866, following repeated petitions and pleas from Texas' government that something be done, General Philip Sheridan wired Governor James Throckmorton that additional military troops had been ordered to the state and that as much protection as possible would be "cheerfully given" to the frontier.[7]

In July of 1866 Frederick P. Sawyer, who had served as a partner in a highly successful East Texas stage line, was granted a contract to carry the mail over the San Antonio to El Paso route, which now ran by way of the Upper Road. His coaches traveled with armed civilian guards. The Indians, however, were not intimidated and continued to attack the mail with impunity. When the stage that left El Paso on February 11 was captured by Kickapoos, the San Antonio *Herald* pleaded for help. "This is not the first mail that has been lost on this line. We hope it will not be much longer before the military afford that protection which is so necessary."[8]

Ben Ficklin joined Sawyer's line that fall and was placed in charge of the operations between San Antonio and El Paso. He built several new stations and improved some of the old ones, including four that came under the protective sphere of Fort

Davis. But with that post in the process of being rebuilt, it was impossible to give as much attention to guard the mail stages as was needed.

In December the post's commander, Colonel Wesley Merritt, authorized mounted escorts of half-dozen of his Ninth Cavalrymen to each coach. They would pick up the stage traveling east and accompany it as far as Barrilla Springs whereupon they joined the westbound stage back to the post. It worked the other direction as well; the escort accompanied the westbound coach as far as Eagle Springs then returned with the eastbound.[9]

Even then the coaches continued to be attacked. No sooner had Colonel Merritt initiated his protection service than an eastbound coach with an eight-man escort was swarmed upon near Eagle Springs by a large party of Apaches. One private was killed and most likely all would have been lost had the coach not made it to the springs where a company under Captain Henry Carroll was camped.[10]

Having a military escort was not always a guarantee of protection. In 1877 the westbound stage arrived at the Fort Davis station and picked up an escort of two soldiers. Near El Muerto Station, the party was jumped by Indians and driver E. P. Webster gave the mules their heads. During the ensuing chase and exchange of fire, one of the soldiers thought safety the better part of valor and decided to trade his horse for the relative security of the stagecoach. As he jumped from his mount to the vehicle and clambered inside, he lost his gun. His action was considered inexcusable and he was drummed out of the army.[11]

By March of 1868 the entire road was protected by thirteen companies of infantry and twenty-four companies of cavalry stationed at six forts, six picket stations, and half a dozen other areas, including mail stations.

Colonel Merritt also began providing guards at stations that continued to be attacked. In December fourteen men were posted at Barrel Springs and eighteen at El Muerto. Merritt was satisfied with the arrangement and in a letter to the Headquarters of the Fifth Military District, reported, "This arrangement of Guards on this line will I think be a thorough protection against Indians in this direction."[12]

Later commanders of Fort Davis offered a different solution to the problem. Believing that the best defense is a good offense, the cavalry began a relentless pursuit of the hostiles, thus restricting their freedom of movement. But when the post's garrison reached a low of 110 enlisted men in February of 1872, Lieutenant Colonel William R. Shafter had to reduce the number of men leaving the post to guard the mail road. He decided to send one trooper per coach directly from Fort Davis and explained his plan in a letter to Major A. P. Morrow at Fort Quitman.

"I believe it has been the practice heretofore for the stage escorts to be furnished from the stations. This I do not approve and am furnishing escorts from the Post and send only men enough to guard the station. Heretofore I have only sent my escort [to] Muerto where he met your escort. Hereafter I will send him till he meets the stage coming down which will be this side of Van Horn's. As you do not, I believe, send any escort above Quitman you will only have one man out part of the time which I suppose you will be able to stand very well. My own post is very small and I have to send down extra and daily duty men as low as possible. We hope to get recruits before long."[13]

Fort Davis eventually got the extra men they needed; the only trouble was that they came from an already undermanned Fort Quitman, leaving that post with but one company. But, even with an extra company of infantry, Fort Davis now had two additional stations to protect, Van Horn's Wells and Eagle Springs, two of the most attacked mail stations on the route.

Shafter's successor Colonel George L. Andrews, who took command of Fort Davis in May of 1872, temporarily discontinued the use of station details. But, later that year, when his superiors at department headquarters heard about this, they ordered him to return the guards to the mail stations between Forts Davis and Quitman.

Reluctantly Andrews set about reinstating the guard details and wrote a letter to Captain Charles Bentzoni, in charge of Fort Quitman, for his advice on numbers of men for each station and their specific duties. "I would also like to know your opinion," Andrews added, "as to whether these guards are not quite as much for the purpose of saving the Stage Company the expense of employing men to take care of their stock as for protection."[14]

In spite of the fact that the military and the stage operators needed each other, the relations between the two were often strained, sometimes to the point of violence. The underlying problem was partly racial and partly bad feelings held over from the war.

Most of the stage men were Southerners, many having served in the Confederacy, while the majority of the soldiers were Union veterans. To make matters worse, troopers from postwar Fort Davis, as well as some other posts, were Negroes. It did not always make for a harmonious partnership. The problem came to a head when station keepers decided to put the black soldiers to work doing menial chores aside from their guard duties.

They were enlisted to help with feeding, grooming, and herding the animals, harnessing teams, and cleaning tack. Without any explicit orders from their superiors to the contrary, the soldiers usually performed them with little protest. Meanwhile, the station keeper at Barrilla Springs displayed a total disdain for the black men in blue. He not only refused them a place to stay, but to feed them as well.[15]

The situation infuriated post commanders. Colonel Shafter wrote a letter to Francis C. Taylor, an agent with the Ben Ficklin company, strongly protesting such treatment.

"I shall be glad to furnish Mail Escorts, as long as they are wanted, but they must be properly treated. They should either be fed by the Company or allowed facilities at the stations for cooking their own rations, a decent place to stay in while at the stations and invariably brought back by the first return stage."[16]

The problem remained unsolved over the years for, in 1880, Lieutenant Colonel John E. Ward of Fort Davis wrote to a noncommissioned officer, part of the guard detail at Barrilla Springs: "It has come to the attention of the Commanding Officer that your detachment is often called upon to do other than guard duty. The duties of your detachment are strictly guard duties, and you will not perform any other duties for anyone, except on orders from these Headquarters."[17]

The racial problem wasn't any better aboard the coaches than it was at the stations. Some drivers turned down black escorts altogether; others refused to return the Negro guards to their posts. Sometimes, an already volatile situation boiled over, as it did at Barrilla Springs in 1873.

During the run between Leon Springs and Barrilla Springs stations, the driver got into a heated argument with his escort, Private Frank Tall of the Twenty-fifth Infantry, and actually struck the trooper in the face. At the station, the driver was in such a foul mood that he cursed one of the soldiers who offered to help harness the fresh team, then drew his revolver and followed Private Tall as the latter walked toward his quarters. The driver fired and missed. Tall turned around, fired, and killed the stage man.[18]

The bad feelings were not always prompted by the stage men. Drivers refused to allow one Private George Taylor to ride with them because of the man's obnoxious behavior. And at Barrilla Springs the situation got so bad in 1880, because of the conduct of the guard detail, that none of the drivers would allow them to escort the coaches without direct orders from the company superintendent. In the subsequent *quid pro quo* that followed, the commanding officer at Fort Davis refused to permit the mail to be carried on any stagecoach that did not have an escort.[19]

Less disastrous, but still one with far reaching ramifications, was the situation that developed at Fort Concho in the summer of 1868. Ironically, the San Antonio *Herald* had praised the cooperation between the mail company and the army less than a month before the onset of hostilities.

"The El Paso road," the article began, "is naturally one of the finest . . . in the world, and with this efficient military protection, will be safe from Indian depradations [sic]. The general management for the protection of the line from the Concho up, is under the immediate supervision of Bvt. Maj. General Edward Hatch, Col. 9th U.S. Cav'y. We have been informed that Major-Gen. J. J. Reynolds, Command'g officer of Texas, is very much interested in the success of this line . . . and will see that nothing is wanting to insure safety along the route . . . ."[20]

The bad blood began not long after Ben Ficklin located a new station near the post. How it started is not entirely clear, but it seemed to have had something to do with the mail company's mules being shod by the army's farrier, supposedly as a favor to the company. At least that was Ficklin's understanding. When Ficklin offered the blacksmith a dollar tip, the latter demanded $25 for the four days' work. Ficklin went to the post commander, Major George C. Cram, who sided with the smithy.[21]

Then we have Major Cram's side of the story which charged Ben Ficklin with "grossly insolent and disrespectful" behavior and for using army property for the mail company's own use.[22]

The Civil War had been over only three years, not nearly long enough to mollify old grudges between the Virginian and any man wearing Union blue. Ficklin, an ex-Confederate himself, accused Cram of purposely delaying the coaches by the post's adjutant not having their mail pouches ready on time and ordered his drivers to adhere to the company's schedule, with or without the army's mail. The feud came to a head when Ficklin's coach departed without the army mail once too often. Cram had the stagecoach stopped and the driver and conductor thrown into the guardhouse.

Ficklin stormed into Cram's office and offered to take his men's place in the guardhouse. Cram was all too happy to oblige. But when the major sought support from his superior and issued an ultimatum that the mail company get a new superintendent or Fort Concho a new commanding officer,

Cram was shocked by Colonel Edward Hatch's order to release the stage man.[23] Ben Ficklin and Frederick Sawyer, the mail line's operator, must have had considerably more influence in Washington than did one of the government's own officers. By summer, Cram had been ordered to another post. He retired five months later.[24]

A military telegraph line was completed along the El Paso road in 1879 and the military grew less dependent upon the stagecoaches. When the Southern Pacific finished laying track across the Trans-Pecos, the U.S. government issued the mail contract to the rail company. In March of 1881 the guard details along the road to El Paso were called back to Fort Davis for the last time.[25]

Notes, Chapter Six

1. Letters Sent. Lt. Col. William R. Shafter to Agent F. C. Taylor, ca. January 1872. Roll No. 1777, Fort Davis NHS. In Douglas McChristian, "Military Protection for the U.S. Mail: A Fort Davis Texas Case Study." 11.
2. Robert M. Utley, *Fort Davis National Historic Site, Texas,* National Park Service Historical Handbook Series No. 38; Washington, D.C., 1965.
3. Missouri *Republican,* 16 November 1858.
4. Waterman L. Ormsby, *The Butterfield Overland Mail,* 50, 93.
5. *Fort Concho Military History of Post,* 206:81. In Carl Coke Rister, *The Southwestern Frontier—1865-1881,* 242.
6. Letters Sent. Fort Davis. Col. Washington Seawell to Commander, Fort Clark. U.S. Regular Army Mobile Units, 1821-1942, N.A. RG 391.
7. San Antonio *Herald,* 16 October 1866.
8. Ibid., 24 February 1867.
9. Douglas C. McChristian, "Apaches and Soldiers: Mail Protection in West Texas," *The Journal of the Council on America's Military Past,* 5.
10. Ibid., 6.
11. Barry Scobee, *Old Fort Davis,* 67.
12. Letters Sent. Fort Davis. Lt. Col. Wesley Merritt to Capt. C. E. Morse, December 22, 1868. U.S. Army Commands, R.G. 98, N.A. Roll No. (7675) 6, Fort Davis NHS. In McChristian, 6-7.
13. Ibid. Lt. Col. William R. Shafter to Maj. A. P. Morrow, February 7, 1872. U.S. Army Commands, R.G. 98, N.A. Roll No. 1777, Fort Davis NHS. In McChristian, 7-8.
14. Ibid. Col. George L. Andrews to Capt. Charles Bentzoni, October 6, 1872. U.S. Army Commands, R.G. 98, N.A. Roll No. 1777, Fort Davis NHS. In McChristian, 8-9.
15. McChristian, 10-11.
16. Letters Sent. Fort Davis. Lt. Col. William R. Shafter to Agent F. C. Taylor. N.A. Roll No. 1777. Fort Davis NHS. In McChristian, 11.
17. Ibid. 1st Lt. W. H. W. James to Non-Commissioned Officer, Barrilla Springs, August 7, 1880, R.G. 98, N.A. Roll (10427) 1. Fort Davis NHS.
18. McChristian, 11-12.

19. Ibid., 11.
20. San Antonio *Daily Herald*, 18 April 1868.
21. Ibid., 13 May 1868; San Antonio *Daily Express*, 14 May 1868. In Wayne R. Austerman, *Sharps Rifles and Spanish Mules*, 214-215.
22. Letters Sent. Fort Concho. Maj. George C. Cram to Col. Edward Hatch, 9 May 1868. R.G. 98, NARS. In Austerman, 215.
23. Ibid., 25 May 1868. In Austerman, 215-216.
24. *Military History of Texas and the Southwest*, Stephen W. Schmidt, Ed., 12:147. In Austerman, 216.
25. McChristian, 15.

CHAPTER SEVEN
"Don't imagine for a moment you are going on a pic-nic"

"I know now what hell is, for
I have had twenty-four days of it."[1]

At Colbert's Ferry on the Red River, five days since leaving St. Louis, Waterman Ormsby penned a letter to his paper, the New York *Herald* and, while he had lost none of the *esprit de corps* he had indicated earlier, he decided he would rather not go without eating to help the mail along.

"We have the strongest hopes of reaching San Francisco in less than the twenty-five days [contract time]. I find roughing it on the plains agrees with me, so that I guess I could go without eating or sleeping for a week. I hope I shan't have to try it, though."[2]

Ormsby tempered his enthusiasm by warning his New York readers that the trip would not be as pleasant "as in a Fourth Avenue car, or the fare as excellent as that of the Astor House, or the climate and temperature as agreeable as the shady side of Broadway in September . . . ."[3]

Mark Twain learned that he would have to make do without some of his accustomed fineries as he boarded the coach in St. Joseph, Missouri, bound for Nevada. Because of the company's twenty-five-pound weight limit of baggage per passenger, Twain and his brother were forced to leave their trunks behind.

"It was a sad parting," he wrote facetiously, "for now we had no swallow-tail coats and white kid gloves to wear at Pawnee receptions in the Rocky Mountains, and no stove-pipe hats nor patent-leather boots, nor anything else necessary to make life calm and peaceful."[4]

While awaiting an available eastbound Butterfield stage in San Francisco, William Tallack had time to reflect upon his decision to go overland rather than by steamer which had been his intention. He said he had been influenced by the promise of "scenic variety and novelty," but expressed some misgiving over the prospects of a "continuous ride of five hundred and forty hours, with no other intermission than a stoppage of about forty minutes twice a day, and a walk, from time to time, over the more difficult ground . . . ."[5] Tallack was right about the walking. Often, a stretch of heavy sand or mud was encountered over which a coach, heavily laden with mail and riders, could not be pulled. At these times, the passengers were required to get out and "walk a spell." Those "Hints for Plains Travelers" had good advice on this subject: "When the driver asks you to get off and walk, do it without grumbling. He will not request it unless absolutely necessary."[6]

Crowded coaches, short tempers, and duels in the sun made for good stories. But the average stagecoach trip was marked by boredom. In fact, many passengers might have longed for a shootout or a spicy love triangle on board to liven things up.

Nathanial Taylor rode over the San Antonio-El Paso mail road in the 1870s and found the tedium unbearable. "Bowled onward and bowled onward," he wrote, "sleeping little or none. It takes one who has the toughness of a light-wood knot to stand this."[7]

"Bowled on and bowled on," he entered in his journal a couple of days later, "night after night and day after day, at last reaching San Antonio after five days and five nights of continual travel, prostrated, collapsed, and used up; felt that I had been dragged through briars and beaten with soot bags . . . felt worse than he who cometh off a drunk."[8]

William Banning, an old stage man himself, said that passengers traveling overland on the San Antonio-San Diego road had to accept the monotonous bounce and sway of the stagecoach as part of "a relentless continuity, a going-on forever and ever. All that was seemed always to have been. And it would continue unceasingly."[9]

The eastern portion of the central routes contributed to a madness of monotony. For six days and some 500 miles, the prairie rolled on and on, without so much as a tree to break its continuity. Even the Platte River, which was met westbound 253 miles into the journey didn't "skirt its bank with timber," wrote a Pennsylvania newspaperman named Alexander McClure. Passengers were always delighted when an infrequent wagon train of emigrants or freight was encountered.

Frank Root, an express messenger with the Central Overland, said that travelers tried to amuse themselves in a variety of ways over this stretch. Gambling was common, although the stage company tried to discourage it. They sang; hymns were a favorite, but they also belted out patriotic pieces and comic songs. If there was a good storyteller among them, he could keep them entertained for hours. If it was the Fourth of July someone always delivered a nationalistic broadside.[10] Most comments, or complaints as the case may be, had to do with the roads. If they weren't too rough, they were too smooth.

"The road, as a whole, from El Paso to Fort Smith," wrote an eastbound traveler over the Butterfield in November of 1858, "possesses a sameness that is really tiresome to the rider."[11]

Ormsby was not impressed with the road that Captain Pope had blazed up the Pecos River on his well-digging expedition in 1855 and wished that the captain could ride in his coach. The jolting, Ormsby described, was "almost interminable and insufferable."[12]

Bad roads could set passengers' tempers on edge as they did with William Tallack's traveling companions after leaving

San Francisco in October of 1858. At Visalia, Tallack and his fellow passengers were transferred to another coach, ". . . with Wild Vic for our driver," he wrote, "who carried us along to the next stopping place—making sixteen miles in one hour and sixteen minutes. This was night driving with a vengeance, and such a growling among the passengers was never heard, as their heads were unceremoniously knocked against the staves that composed the framework of the cover. The road was rough, the night dark, the mustangs wild, and all out of humor . . . ."[13]

Nineteenth century wayfarers were not immune to some of the problems that plague travelers today. H. C. Logan found his co-passengers' nerves a bit jangled when they had to switch coaches at night between the Llano and Concho rivers in Texas. "The temper of the passengers," he wrote, "was marred a little by the necessity of changing coaches, transferring mail, baggage, etc. in the middle of a muddy prairie, in freezing weather about three o'clock in the morning."[14]

One would think that such rustic traveling would not contribute to one's good health, yet some swore that an overland journey would cure whatever ailed you.

In November of 1860 Albert Richardson, a Boston journalist who made several trips over more than one overland route, shared an eastbound coach from Denver with two living testimonials. One was a widow who just ten days before was near death from typhoid fever. "At starting," he wrote, "she was still an invalid, and the ride of the first day and night left her hardly able to sit up. But in the inspiring, pure air of the plains she rallied, gained an enormous appetite; and before the end of the trying six days and nights her cheeks again were the bloom of health." The other passenger, a seventy-year-old man, was also an invalid. For the first two days on the road he was too weak to get out of the coach and his meals had to be brought to him. "But, he too gained wonderful strength before reaching the river."[15]

The *Texas Almanac* of 1859 praised the trip over the San Antonio-San Diego route, sounding somewhat like a twentieth century tour guide. The writer described the "fine, natural roads" over which the average speed was six miles per hour. "Respecting the accommodations," the treatise went on, "they are as good as circumstances will admit, the stages being so arranged that passengers can recline in them comfortably, and take their sleep whilst traveling. The provisions are the best that nature of so long a trip will allow. The character of the country is that of a high, dry, and eminently healthy one and a trip across the continent could hardly fail to prove beneficial to the health of the traveler."[16]

Phocion Way, who journeyed over most of that route in the spring and early summer of 1858, would have argued with the *Almanac's* description of "fine, natural roads" following his experience at the infamous Lancaster Hill. During Way's time, a new road was being cut in the side of the mountain which would knock about six miles off the previous route. But, it wasn't yet finished and was no less tortuous than the old one.

"We were induced to try it last night to save time," Way wrote, "but such a road! I have heard of dangerous roads, but I never saw one like this. We were compelled to descend at least half a mile down the side of a rugged mountain over loose stones and large rocks . . . it is not yet ready for the passage of wagons, but we did not know that." Way and his fellow passengers had to pitch in to remove rocks from the road. Then, with the coach's brakes locked, all held on to the wheels as the vehicle was inched down bit by bit.[17]

Weather attributed to a great deal of passengers' discomforts. During the summer, heat inside a coach could rise to 110 degrees or more. Male passengers would often sleep on the roofs [impossible with the canvas-topped Celeritys], tying themselves to the rails to keep from falling off. In the deserts or plains, dust, often mixed with alkali, was kicked up by the team's hooves and entered the coach through the slightest of cracks even with the shades lowered.

By all accounts, the worst traveling lay across the deserts during the summer.

Mark Twain had looked forward to seeing a western Sahara. The opportunity came 190 miles west of Salt Lake City when his coach entered a stretch of Nevada wasteland 68 miles across, with a water stop about two-thirds of the way through. The first 45 mile stretch was covered in the dark. It was sunrise when they stopped to water the team and Twain was delighted with the idea of crossing the next 23 miles in daylight. "This was fine—novel—romantic—dramatically adventurous—*this*, indeed, was worth living for, worth traveling for!"[18]

But his fervor wilted as quickly as his body, lasting barely an hour under the August sun. "Imagine a vast, waveless ocean," he wrote, "stricken dead and turned to ashes... imagine a coach, creeping like a bug through the midst of this shoreless level... imagine this aching monotony of toiling and plowing kept up hour after hour... imagine team, driver, coach, and passengers so deeply coated with ashes that they are all one colorless color... This is the reality of it."[19] After ten hours of breathing alkali and suffering parched lips, Twain had lost his usual wit, not to mention his enthusiasm. "... truly and seriously the romance all faded far away and disappeared, and left the desert trip nothing but a harsh reality —a thirsty, sweltering, longing, hateful reality!"[20]

It wasn't the last badlands encountered. In Nevada, Twain described the "Great American Desert—forty memorable miles of bottomless sand, into which the coach wheels sunk from six inches to a foot. We worked our passage most of the way across. That is to say, we got out and walked." Bordering this desert, which was so littered with the bones of oxen and horses that they could have walked the entire distance without stepping on land, was the Carson Sink, "a shallow, melancholy sheet of water some eighty or a hundred miles in circumference."[21]

Albert Richardson could have warned Mr. Twain about the alkali and sand coating everything. Before departing upon his trip across Nevada, this 'frequent traveler' had his beard shaved and hair cut short. He explained: "This lessens the disagreeableness of the alkaline dust which envelops horses and drivers, vehicle and inmates."[22]

"Old Stagecoach of the Plains," by Frederic Remington. Like most stage lines, this coach is running at night, keeping to a 24-hour a day schedule. Those operators who did not run around the clock, did not have to order the side lamps, which cost extra. (Courtesy Amon Carter Museum)

William Tallack was another overland chronicler who could have done without desert traveling. After rolling across the barren plain between Carrizo and the Colorado River, he wrote: "Hour after hour we were enveloped in clouds of fine clayey dust . . . What with the hot wind, the dust, and the perspiration, our faces and hands became covered with a thin mud . . . ."[23]

Not all curses had to do with sand and alkali. Mosquitoes along the Platte River were regular man-eaters and could so cover your face that you were made unrecognizable by your companions. Perhaps even worse were the tiny sand gnats that found their way in your hair and under clothing with a bite that some said were worse than the mosquitoes.[24]

Stagecoaches rolled on regardless of the weather and winter could be as much a hardship as summer. Nathanial Taylor experienced a good old Texas "blue norther" at Barrilla Springs.

"At eleven o'clock [P.M.]," he wrote, "a furious norther suddenly leaped in the window of the stagecoach, and saluted us with a whiff of its frozen breath. Instantly the windows were closed, and I wrapped myself up in overcoat and blankets, but notwithstanding all the weight of wool, I shivered and suffered terribly . . . . For much of the way we rode athwart this torrent; and it shrieked and howled among the iron and leather fixtures of the coach."[25]

A welcome addition to the winter inventory of a stagecoach was a foot-stove that was filled at the stations with sand and live coals, heated brick, or soapstone. The stove was then tucked in under the passengers' feet. The men on the box also had a foot warmer. Wrapped with blankets and buffalo robes and with heat at their feet, drivers and passengers alike could only hope that the next station was reached before the little stoves turned cold.

The proponents of both of the "temperate" southern routes might have been just a little red-faced during the winters of 1858 and 1859. Ice coated the Rio Grande at El Paso in January. One mail took thirty days to make it to San Antonio from San Diego due to heavy snow in the canyons of the Devil's River in southwest Texas, and just the month before, W. Beardsley of Arizona suffered frozen feet in Apache Pass as he and his fellow passengers were forced to walk twelve miles in snow 2½ feet deep.[26]

Thunderstorms could pop up in an instant. Demas Barnes, traveling over the Central Overland route in the summer of 1865, had tired of sitting in a stifling hot coach and was relieved when the driver invited him to sit on the box. That is, until a violent prairie thunderstorm blew up. ". . . the wind rose to a hurricane that seemed about to snap and start the very sods from the earth, while as to rain—it might have rained harder before, and it might have rained harder since, but I didn't happen to be out in it. A ship might as well proceed under full sail in a typhoon, as a stage across the plains in one of these storms."[27]

Spring and summer weather on the Kansas and Nebraska prairies could be horrendous. Sometimes the wind was so strong that it shook the coaches, staggered the teams, and blew luggage away. In the summer, prairie fires were not uncommon and the coach would have to crawl through choking smoke for miles. If the wind suddenly shifted, it was a hell-bent-for-leather race to save lives.

Not all travelers found inclement weather so distressing. Just after entering Texas during his westbound journey in the summer of 1859, Albert Richardson reported that his coach met the "California mail, with six smoking horses on a swift run through the drenching rain, and the passengers lustily singing . . . .'Down upon the Suwanee river'."[28]

The wind blew hard enough through Guadalupe Pass one November day in 1858 to rip the bridles from the mules' heads. "We took our seats in the coach with unpleasant forebodings of a disagreeable night in store for us . . . ." wrote one of the riders. The comfort of the vehicle did not last long. In the teeth of the tempest, the passengers were asked to walk if they hoped to reach the Pinery Station. At the summit they encountered a brief, but fierce, snowstorm.[29]

One of the major complaints from overland travelers was the company's exclusive use of mules throughout Texas and the southwest. Horses pulled Butterfield's coaches on both ends, and "Admiral John" obviously had them in mind when he instructed his employees on the proper method to change teams at the stations:

"Have teams harnessed in ample time, and ready to proceed without delay or confusion. Teams should be hitched together and led to or from the stable to the coach, so that no delay can occur by their running away."[30]

It sounded great in theory. But Mister Butterfield was more accustomed to the civilized, well-trained horses of the east and not the animals which were subsequently asked to drag his coaches over the wilds of the southwest.

At Diamond's Station, the next stop upon leaving Sherman, Waterman Ormsby witnessed his first wild mules being harnessed to a stagecoach and described the incident blow by blow.

First the mules had to be secured with a rope to a tree or post, ". . . then the harness had to be put on piece by piece, care being taken to avoid his teeth and heels. Altogether, I should estimate the time consumed in the process at not less than half an hour to each wild mule, and that, when the mail has to wait for it, might, I think, much better be spent on the road . . . I was much amused with the process, but it seemed a little behind the age for the mail to wait for it . . . ."[31]

Ormsby was not so amused by a similar scene at Fort Chadbourne. He had remained in the coach while the relay team was harnessed, upon which the animals commenced to throw fits. "The mules," he wrote, "reared, pitched, twisted, whirled, wheeled, ran, stood still, and cut up all sorts of capers. The wagon performed so many evolutions that I, in fear of my life, abandoned it and took to my heels, fully confident that I could make more progress in a straight line, with much less risk of breaking my neck." Ormsby made the right decision, for the top of the coach was demolished. "I thought it the most ludicrous scene I ever witnessed . . . ."[32]

Albert Richardson had an even scarier time after leaving Fort Davis with four half-broken mules in the traces. The team was unmanageable and at one point, when the coach teetered on two wheels and seemed in imminent danger of capsizing, Richardson bailed out. It took the driver a mile to turn the vehicle around and come back for him. One of his fellow passengers, an army colonel, admonished him for abandoning the coach. "You are fortunate to escape a broken neck," the officer told him. "Whatever happens, always stick to the coach," to which another passenger, a general, added, "And *never* jump out over a wheel!"[33]

Not long afterward, the mules again transformed the coach "into a pitching schooner, which the bounding billows of prairie tossed and rolled and threatened to wreck," wrote Richardson. "I kept in the vehicle; but both my military companions jumped headlong over a hind-wheel to the sure and firm-set earth." The colonel suffered a sprained ankle, the general a badly bruised foot and both had their "own wise counsel . . . repeated to them."[34]

John Butterfield's perfect team-changing scenario notwithstanding, the way it really went was something like this: The arriving coach would drive into the corral and be turned pointing in the direction of the open gate. The wild team was harnessed and let go, and the mules commenced to run full bore to the next station. At least, such was Raphael Pumpelly's experience.

"At several stations," he began, "six wild horses [mules] were hitched blindfolded into their places. When everything was ready, the blinds were removed at a signal from the driver, and the animals started off at a run-away speed, which they kept up without slackening till the next station, generally twelve miles distant. In these cases the driver had no further control over his animals than the ability to guide them; to stop, or even check them, was entirely beyond his power . . . Nothing but the most perfect presence of mind on the part of the driver could prevent accidents."[35]

Woe betide the passenger whose nature call could not wait until the next station. Nathanial Taylor said that, in these situations, ". . . the best the driver can do is to rein the mules out of the road and keep the coach whirling in a circle. The passenger must get out and back again at imminent risk of breaking his bones."[36]

All the meticulous work and care that the eastern coach builders put into their products could not have prepared them for the rigors of western use or save a coach from the energetic driving of the western "Jehus," who, after all, were only complying with company rules such as these from John Butterfield:

"Every person in the Company's employ will always bear in mind that each minute of time is of importance. If each driver on the route loses fifteen (15) minutes, it would make a total loss of time, on the entire route, of twenty-five (25) hours, or more than one day."

"All hands will see the great necessity of promptness and dispatch: every minute of time is valuable as the Company are under heavy forfeit if the mail is behind time."[37]

Waterman Ormsby experienced the results of some energetic driving early on in his pioneer journey. On September 19, his fourth night on the road, the coach was being driven at an alarming rate over a tortuous road that found him bouncing on the seat, against the roof, into the side. Something had to give and it did. Two hard thumps unseated Ormsby and his companions. An examination at the next station revealed a broken tongue. "It took more time to mend it than the ambitious driver saved," he wrote. "Moral—'Make haste slowly'."[38]

Hiram Rumfield, a Butterfield agent at the Fort Smith office during the company's southern service, was well aware of the dangerous roads through the Ozarks and the relish with which the drivers obeyed the company's policy toward speed and wrote in a letter to his wife on the 22d of June 1860, that anyone "who can pass over this route a passenger in one of the Overland Mail Coaches, without experiencing feelings of mingled terror and astonishment, must certainly be oblivious to every consideration of personal safety."[39]

Despite the great care in its design, the stagecoach, particularly the heavy Concord or Troy, was basically top-heavy. Overturning was the most common accident along the road and the coaches did so frequently.

One vehicle overturned twice west of Yuma, Arizona, and again east of Van Buren, Arkansas. Another eastbound coach overturned near Fort Chadbourne and while it was being righted, the westbound arrived on the scene and it promptly turned over. One passenger aboard the latter suffered a broken shoulder.[40] Injuries were common. Raphael Pumpelly recalled meeting an eastbound coach in which every one of its passengers had a bandaged head or an arm in a sling.[41]

Runaway teams were among the most common causes of overturned coaches. A driver had few recourses in his bag of tricks to use in stopping a runaway stagecoach. One was applying the brake full force; but if it didn't work quickly enough, the brake beam was likely to snap. Sometimes, the driver would throw his right leg over the reins while bracing his left against the footboard. The additional leverage worked well on sore mouthed horses or mules and frequently prevented a spill.[42]

The biggest worry one had with a coach turning over was its being dragged by the team. Were it not for a simple design, many more passengers and drivers would have most certainly been killed in such accidents. To prevent the vehicle from being dragged, the kingpin that held the frame to the tongue assembly worked by gravity so that it would fall out when the coach went on its side, thereby releasing the team.

On this subject, a passenger on a Sawyer and Risher coach between Austin, Texas, and San Antonio in December of 1859 reported that his ride was made "a little more spicy by the upsetting of the stage coach, about ten miles beyond this city [Austin] . . . We were all rolling on as finely as a heart could wish, when all at once something appeared to tickle the horses, and the next we knew, we were turned up in one promiscous [sic] heap . . .

"As the coach turned [over] the kingbolt . . . at once flew out, this separated the body of the stage from the forward wheels, and prevented the horses . . . from dragging the coach upon its side, and perhaps killing its inmates."[43]

But even the best of designs failed to work now and then. The coach that arrived in San Antonio from Alleyton on September 23, 1867, did so with an overly flamboyant driver in the box. He took the turn into the square much too short and the vehicle capsized, throwing him from his seat. The kingpin did not immediately respond to Newton's Law and the vehicle was dragged for some distance before finally disengaging. No one aboard the stagecoach was injured, but some women in a buggy rammed by the frightened team were.[44]

Accidents could be caused by other reckless souls on the road then as now. Between Waco and Houston, several drunken riders dashed by the stage and spooked the horses into bolting down a hill. The coach was upset, throwing the driver off the box and breaking his thigh. A passenger was also hurt, two horses killed, and the coach broken to pieces.[45]

Rivers posed particular hazards on the mail roads, there being few bridges or ferries. Coaches could be upset even in normal currents and were often lost. In August of 1880 a stagecoach was swept away by a flooded Limpia Creek and when it was found seventy-two hours later, the driver was dead and the mail a "mass of pulp."[46]

But the rivers didn't necessarily have to be high. Mark Twain concluded that he and his companions were sure goners when they became mired in quicksand while fording the shallow South Platte River in Colorado. Twain lent the situation his usual sardonic wit. "Once or twice in midstream," he wrote, "the wheels sunk into the yielding sands so threateningly that we half believed we had dreaded and avoided the sea all our lives to be shipwrecked in a 'mudwagon' in the middle of a desert."[47]

Tedium was the major complaint of overland travelers. One of the methods that bored passengers used to amuse themselves was to take pot shots at any wildlife that had the misfortune of being within range. Buffalo were favorite targets because of their fatal tendency for indifference in the midst of being slaughtered. But the shaggy brutes got their revenge of sorts by exhibiting complete disdain for mail schedules and such. Sometimes, in their peak years, the huge herds could hold up stagecoaches for hours as they meandered across the road.

A correspondent for the San Antonio *Express* experienced such a sight on his journey to El Paso in the spring of 1869. "Wanderer," his *nom de plume*, reported striking large herds of buffalo a few miles west of Fort Concho. "The buffalo are quite tame," he wrote, "often remaining within 25 steps of the road while our coach passed. By stopping the coach I was enabled to stand up and take many shots of the noble fellows at point blank range . . . Thus this night is relieved of its monotony."[48]

It would seem that overland stagecoaching was, as one anonymous traveler put it, "twenty-four days of hell." But such was not always the case. There were moments of utter beauty, such as Ormsby's description of the sight of the Guadalupe Mountains in Trans-Pecos Texas by moonlight. From Pope's Camp, sixty miles away, Ormsby saw them standing "in bold relief against the clear sky, like the walls of some ancient fortress covered with towers and embattlements."[49]

Many passengers shared moments like these at one time or another along the roads and, at journey's end, looked back on their trips with satisfaction.

Ormsby assured would-be travelers over the Butterfield route that they would be relieved "from all danger from sea-sickness and the dull monotony of a sea voyage; they can travel by comfortable stages, stopping at such interesting points as they may choose for rest, and enjoying many opportunities for viewing the beautiful, the wonderful, and the sublime products of nature . . . ."[50]

Unlike some of his contemporaries, Ormsby did not find the journey monotonous or perilous. ". . . throughout the whole 2,700 miles," he wrote, "the interest in new objects is not allowed to flag . . . if this trip may be considered a criterion, the alleged danger from Indians is all a bugbear." He said he felt fresh enough to make the journey again, although he did not specify when. At any rate, he took a steamer back to New York.[51]

Our honeymooners, the H. D. Barrows, perhaps by the very nature of their trip, found their jaunt on the Southern Overland highly enjoyable.

"Of course the journey was somewhat tedious," Mr. Barrows admitted, "but this was more than compensated for by the incidents and variety of scenery of the vast stretch of country passed through, and really, the weariness of stage travel was less disagreeable, than sea-sickness, etc., by water, as we had occasion to realize on our return trip, by way of the Isthmus."[52]

H. C. Logan enjoyed his journey over the San Antonio-west route but tempered his enthusiasm with a warning for those would-be travelers expecting to find all the comforts of home. ". . . we would say that if any man has business on the western frontier requiring his attention, and regards time as money, let him take the El Paso stage—he will find as much comfort as is generally had in such lines of communication. The tourist from whatever clime he may come, may see much to wonder at that he never saw before; but if he expects ease and luxury . . . he will find himself disappointed."[53]

Demas Barnes found nothing gratifying about his own trip and had some good advice for anyone contemplating an overland trek. "Many friends said they envied me my trip, would themselves like to go, etc. I do not doubt their sincerity . . . but I beg to undeceive them. It is not a *pleasant*, but it is an *interesting* trip. The condition of one man's running stages to make money, while another seeks to ride in them for pleasure, are not in harmony to produce comfort. Coaches will be overloaded, it will rain, the dust will drive, baggage will be left to the storm, passengers will get sick . . . children will cry . . . passengers will get angry, the drivers will swear, the sensitive will shrink, rations will give out . . . the water brackish, the whiskey abominable, and the dirt almost unendurable. I have just finished six days and nights of this thing; and I am free to say . . . I shall not undertake it again."[54]

J. C. Tucker, whose own journey was spiced by the love triangle and subsequent duel, certainly couldn't complain of monotony on his trip. But by the time he arrived in San Francisco, he was so weary that not even being met by E. S. Alvord, the general superintendent of the San Francisco-Los Angeles division (and mistakenly identified by Tucker as vice-president of the stage line), could raise his spirits.

"I much fear that at that time we failed to appreciate his [Alvord's] courtesy. Just then we were happy to arrive, and could admire almost anything—except a stage and a stage-company's president."[58]

William Tallack admitted that his eastbound jaunt was interesting, but was happy to trade the stagecoach for the train at Syracuse, Missouri, then the western terminus for the Pacific Railroad. ". . . never did a ride seem more luxuriously [sic] comfortable than the smooth and rapid motion of the commodious railway-cars, both by their contrast with our three weeks' route over rugged mountain and rolling prairie, as well as by the restful feeling arising from the secure accomplishment of a journey so different from any in our former experiences of travel."[56]

Mark Twain, however, was almost poetic in recounting his 1,800-mile, twenty-day journey to the wild West.

"The stage whirled along at a spanking gait, the breeze flapping curtains and suspended coats in a most exhilarating way; the cradle swayed and swung luxuriously; the pattering of the horses' hoofs, the cracking of the driver's whip, and his 'Hi-yi! g'lang!' were music; the spinning ground and the waltzing trees appeared to give us a mute hurrah as we went by . . . we felt that there was only one complete and satisfying happiness in the world, and we had found it."[57]

Twain could be thankful, according to the "Hints for Plains Travelers." That article ended its dictates on proper behavior on the road by warning readers not to "imagine for a moment you are going on a pic-nic; expect annoyance, discomfort and some hardships. If you are disappointed, thank heaven."[58]

Notes, Chapter Seven

1. J. Marvin Hunter, Ed., "Tragedies of the Old Stage Days," *Frontier Times*, 106.
2. Waterman L. Ormsby, *The Butterfield Overland Mail*, 20.
3. Ibid., 141.
4. Mark Twain, *Roughing It*, 3.
5. William Tallack, *The California Overland Express. The Longest Stage-Ride in the World*, 21.
6. Omaha *Herald*, 1877.
7. Col. Nathaniel Alston Taylor, *The Coming Empire, or, Two Thousand Miles in Texas on Horseback*, 360.
8. Ibid., 361.
9. Capt. William Banning and George Hugh Banning, *Six Horses*, 117.
10. Frank A. Root and William Elsey Connelley, *The Overland Stage to California*, 509-510.
11. Walter Barnes Lang, *The First Overland Mail: Butterfield Trail, San Francisco to Memphis, 1858-1861*, 42.
12. Ormsby, 69.
13. Tallack, 70.
14. San Antonio *Daily Herald*, 30 October 1868.
15. Albert D. Richardson, *Beyond the Mississippi*, 324-325. The river mentioned was most likely the Mississippi, which would have been reached after a ride of six days.
16. J. Marvin Hunter, Ed., "Thirty-Day Mail Schedule to California," *Frontier Times*, Vol. 26, No. 9, 219.
17. William A. Duffen, Ed., "Overland Via 'Jackass Mail' in 1858. The Diary of Phocion R. Way," *Arizona and the West*, 47.
18. Twain, 86.
19. Ibid., 86-87.
20. Ibid., 88
21. Ibid., 92.
22. Richardson, 467.
23. Tallack, 35.
24. David Nevin, *The Expressmen*, 166-167.
25. Taylor, 357-358.
26. Missouri *Republican*, 23 December 1858, and 21 January 1859; San Antonio *Herald*, 12 January 1858.
27. Demas Barnes, *From the Atlantic to the Pacific, Overland*, 19-20.

28. Richardson, 225.
29. Lang, *The First Overland Mail, San Francisco to Memphis*, 37.
30. "Special Instructions."
31. Ormsby, 43.
32. Ibid., 54.
33. Richardson, 235.
34. Ibid.
35. Raphael Pumpelly, *Across Asia and America*, 4-5.
36. Taylor, 349.
37. From the "Overland Mail Company. Through Time Schedules. Sept. 16th, 1858."
38. Ormsby, 31, 32.
39. Archer Butler Hulbert, Ed., "Letters of an Overland Mail Agent in Utah. Hiram S. Rumfield Correspondence," 238.
40. Missouri *Republican*, 23 December 1858, and 4 February 1859.
41. Pumpelly, 5.
42. Nick Eggenhofer, *Wagons, Mules and Men. How the Frontier Moved West*, 174.
43. San Antonio *Herald*, 29 December 1859.
44. San Antonio *Express*, 24 September 1867.
45. San Antonio *Herald*, 14 September 1859.
46. Clayton W. Williams, *Texas' Last Frontier. Fort Stockton & the Trans-Pecos, 1861-1895*, 263.
47. Twain, 29.
48. San Antonio *Express*, 14 April 1869.
49. Ormsby, 71,
50. Ibid., 130.
51. Ibid., 59. Ormsby hailed the Overland as "the second greatest event of the age," the first being the laying of the Trans-Atlantic cable a month earlier. He is also said to have ridden the first westbound Union Pacific train in 1869 as a guest reporter of the railroad, although I have found no confirmation of this. He saw many changes in transportation during his life, including airplanes. He died in 1908 at the age of 74.
52. Lang, *The First Overland Mail, San Francisco to Memphis*, 64,
53. San Antonio *Daily Herald*, 24 November 1868.
54. Barnes, 7-8.
55. Dr. Joseph C. Tucker, *To the Golden Goal and Other Sketches*, 198-199.
56. Tallack, 65-66.
57. Twain, 8.
58. Omaha *Herald*, 1877.

CHAPTER EIGHT
"... the most desolate of human habitations"

"It is such a house as I never
saw before I came to Texas ... a
regular backwood establishment."[1]

At Leon Springs Station, west of Fort Stockton, William Tallack expressed surprise at the "refinement" he found there, "very different from the rugged aspect of the generality of Overland stations and their inmates. This was owing to the presence of a cheerful matronly woman ... and two gentle girls, her young daughters, bright 'prairie flowers' not often seen in these rough Far-Western wilds."[2]

While the young English Quaker's choice of the word "inmates" might have been purely by chance, no doubt many stage employees who lived at these remote stations, what Albert Richardson called "... the most desolate and lonely of all human habitations," must have indeed felt like prisoners.[3]

True, there were no bars and one has to assume they were there by choice; but surrounded as they were by hundreds of square miles of wilderness inhabited by hostile Indians, no barred doors or stone walls could have been more confining.

It took a special breed of man, and woman, to live and work at an Eagle Springs or Apache Pass Station, for even the Butterfield employees lived in constant danger. The Indians may have had a hands-off policy when it came to "Chief John's swift-wagons," but there were no such agreements toward the stage stands.

Take Camp Johnston Station for instance. The agent of the lonely stand just west of the Concho River, his three attendants, one of their wives, and her two children were awakened early on the morning of September 2, 1859, by the sounds of a Comanche raiding party. Whooping with glee, the Indians stormed into the corral and, while the residents cowered inside the house, killed a mule and began eating it then and there. Never was the sound of a coach horn more welcome than at that moment. With the stagecoach coming in, the Indians rounded up the remaining mules and made a hasty exit.[4]

In February of 1861 thirty Comanches attacked the same station and stole the stock. One can imagine the surprise of the station keepers when the leader of the raiding party returned a short time later. Speaking in broken English to the agent, Joel Pennington, the Comanche expressed his displeasure over the poor quality of the purloined stock and warned that if the braves didn't find better animals when they returned in another moon, the station would be burned and everyone inside killed.

In a month, the Indians returned as promised but found only a single wagon team and a couple of scrawny ponies. It isn't that Pennington intentionally flirted with danger; Texas had just recently seceded from the Union and the station was being abandoned. The infuriated Comanches didn't take too kindly to the situation, however, and began attacking the quarters. Fortunately, the thick split log walls prevented the arrows from entering the house; unfortunately, the Indians set fire to it, forcing the occupants outside. During the ensuing shootout, Pennington was wounded but the other men managed to repulse the attackers and get help from Fort Chadbourne. Though his wounds were grievous, the agent did recover.[5]

'Overland Station - Indians Coming in With the Stage,' by Frederic Remington. Judging by the number of men at the building, this was probably a home station. (Courtesy Denver Public Library, Western History Department)

STATION DIAGRAMS

The eleven station diagrams, with floor plans and other features, are shown to represent the variety of stage stations along Butterfield's Southern Overland Mail route and include stations in Missouri, Texas, New Mexico, Arizona, Mexico, and California.

All are drawn by the author based on the originals by Roscoe P. Conkling and Margaret B. Conkling and published in *The Butterfield Overland Mail, 1857-1869*, The Arthur H. Clark Company, and with their consent.

The diagrams are not drawn to scale.

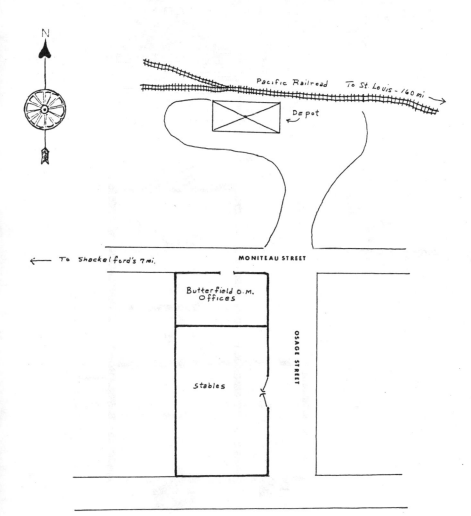

TIPTON, MISSOURI

Terminus Pacific Railroad September 1858

Butterfield station and stable doors, and depot roof added by author. Rest drawn according to Conkling, 1931.

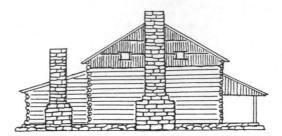

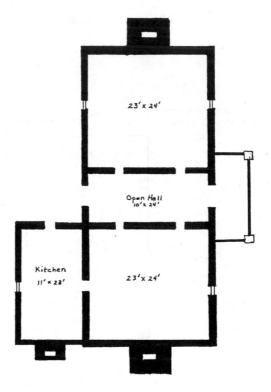

EARHART'S STATION
Jack County, Texas

Home belonged to Joseph B. Earhart, was a story-and-a-half and constructed of double logs. (Per Conkling, 1931).

(Note: hallway doors were not drawn on Conkling's plans but were added on the basis of known designs from that period.)

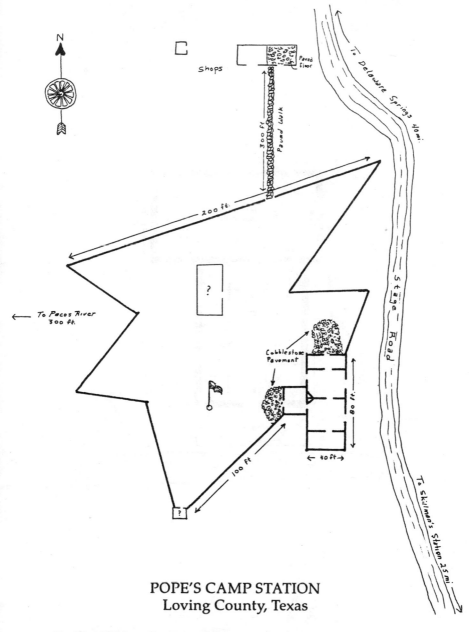

POPE'S CAMP STATION
Loving County, Texas

Built 1855 by Captain John Pope.
Stone and adobe walls. (Per Conkling, 1932.)

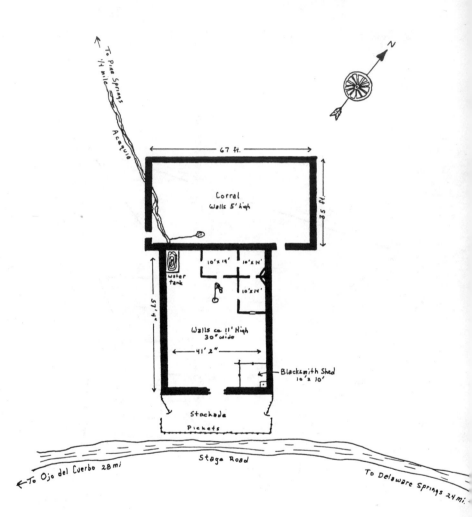

THE PINERY STATION
Culberson County, Texas

Elevation 5,634 feet, highest elevation on original route.
(Per Conkling, 1931.)

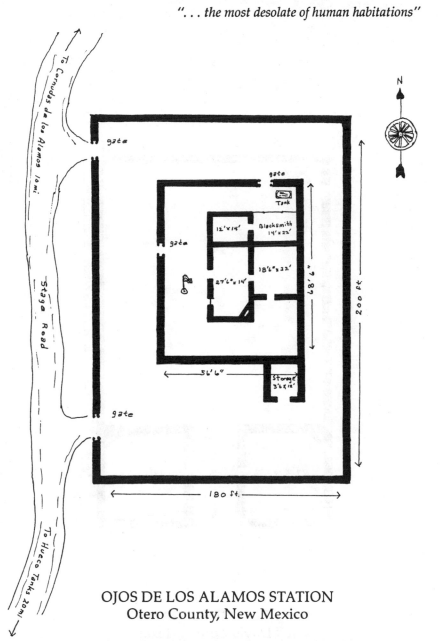

OJOS DE LOS ALAMOS STATION
Otero County, New Mexico

Built of stone. Outer corral walls were 3 feet high. Enclosure walls were 9 feet high, 27 inches thick. (Per Conkling, 1935.)

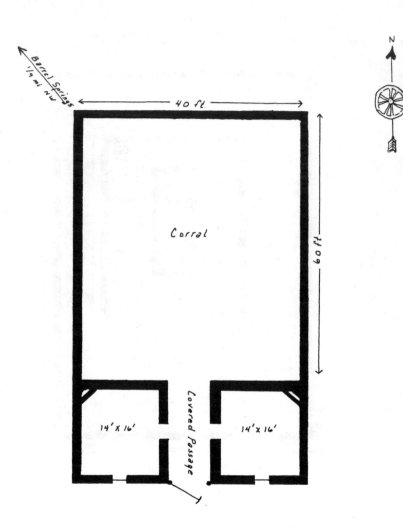

BARREL SPRING STATION
Jeff Davis County, Texas

Rock walls were 9 feet high and 3 feet thick. Elevation about 5,000 feet. (Per Conkling, 1935.)

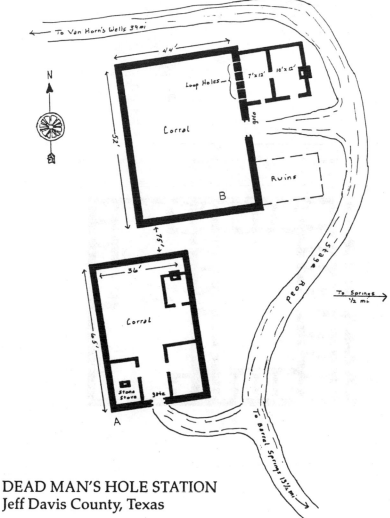

DEAD MAN'S HOLE STATION
Jeff Davis County, Texas

A   Older (Butterfield) station. Constructed of stone.

B   Later (probably Ficklin) station. Corral constructed of stone; the rooms were adobe. Notice the loop holes through which men in room could fire upon Indians in corral.

Stations, elevation ca. 4,500 feet, were located a half mile west of Dead Man's (El Muerto) Spring, in a canyon on north side of El Muerto Peak. (Per Conkling, 1935.)

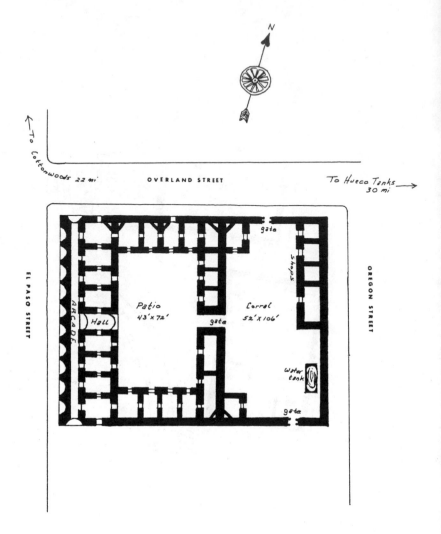

EL PASO STATION
El Paso County, Texas

Adobe. Walls were 20 feet high and nearly 3 feet thick. Built in 1858 by Anson Mills. Razed in 1900. (Per Conkling, no date.)

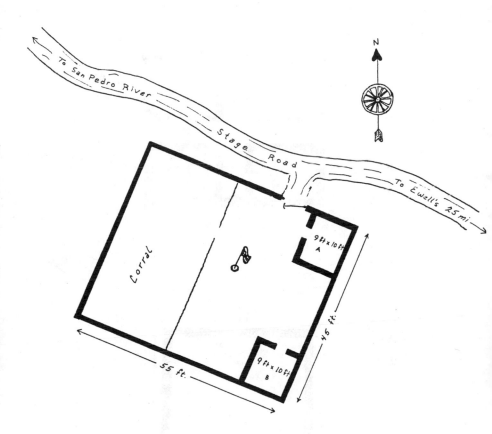

DRAGOON SPRINGS STATION
Cochise County, Arizona

Built of rock slabs. Walls originally 10 feet high, 3 feet thick.

Room A was where Silas St. John was attacked on the night of September 8, 1858.

Room B was where Preston Cunningham was killed.

(Per Conkling, no date.)

117

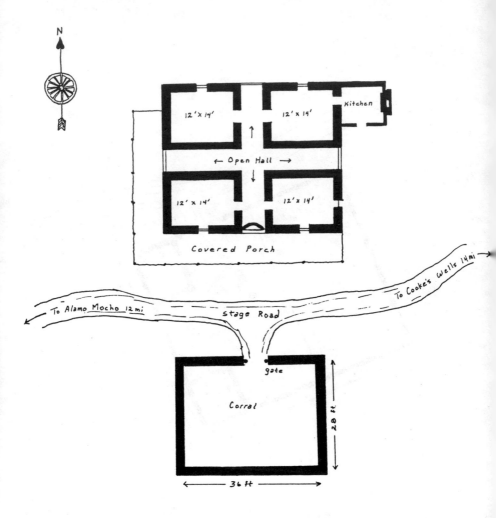

GARDNER'S WELLS STATION
Baja California, Mexico

Walls were of adobe. (Per Conkling, no date.)

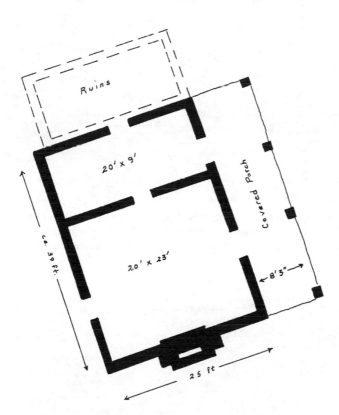

VALLECITO STATION
San Diego County, California

The first structure (dotted lines) was probably built for the Army in 1852.

Walls of the station and porch pillers were 30 inches thick and constructed of sod bricks. Station has been restored.

(Per Conkling, 1927.)

The Butterfield station at El Paso, built in 1858 by Anson Mills, was the most imposing building in town, even in 1868 when this picture was taken. This view of the 12-arch arcade is from El Paso Street. (Courtesy El Paso Public Library)

Unidentified mail station in the Concho country, date unknown. Like all stations throughout the southwest, it was adobe. (Courtesy Wayne R. Austerman)

The Pinery, the Butterfield station as it appeared in 1858, was the highest station on the original route at more than 6,000 feet. It is the only station presently located near a major highway. Its ruins are in Guadalupe Mountains National Park, just south of the Texas-New Mexico state line. (Courtesy National Park Service)

Eagle Springs was no doubt one of the most dangerously situated of the stations in Texas, located in the narrow Eagle Springs Canyon in present Hudspeth County. When the ruins of the station were discovered by the Conklings in the 1930s, the authors reported several grave mounds nearby, evidence of the violence that occurred here all too often. The station was destroyed at least three times in its sanguinary career.[6]

Barrilla Springs Station, where Nathanial Taylor stopped for supper on his overland journey, was described by the author as having a "singularly lonesome and dejected look as if it had lost its mother . . . I perceived that it had an unusually large cemetery for so diminutive a population. It is accounted as a sort of dead-hole, a place of danger, and these graves mark the resting place of travelers or employes of the stage company who were slain by Indians."[7]

Workers at the distant stations could become stranded in extreme weather or other hazards. When their supplies ran out one winter, employees at the Limpia Station had to exist for twelve days on corn ground in a coffee mill.[8]

Not all of the western stage stands were so gloomily situated. Grape Creek Station, 13 miles southwest from the Colorado River in Coke County, Texas, presented a pretty picture to the weary traveler despite its history of Indian harassment. Huge pecan trees shaded the East Branch of Grape Creek where the split log house was located and wild grapes abounded in the area.

At least one station had something of a tourist attraction to offer. Passengers stopping for meals at Hueco Tanks east of El Paso reported looking at the many pictographs on the walls overlooking the natural water basins.[9]

Life at the scattered western stations must have been especially lonely and trying on the women. True, the arrival of a stagecoach was a welcome and frequent diversion; but, unless she lived at a meal station, there were no opportunities to visit with the passengers, most of whom were men anyway. The best she could hope for was that the coach brought letters from home and loved ones or newspapers with all the hometown gossip and social activities. Every now and then, a home station held a dance, or "hop," and women up and down the line would go to the function by any means available, sometimes traveling a hundred miles round trip.[10]

The stations along the Central Route through the mid-1860s were not so different from those in the southwest. The danger from Indian attacks was certainly just as great; Albert Richardson described loop-holes bored through the stone walls of stations and revolvers and rifles hanging at the ready. Yet, most of "the women are comely and lady-like," he wrote, "adapting themselves with grace and heroism to the rude labors of cooking meals for passengers, and the horrible, ever-present peril of capture."[11]

The remote stations offering no amenities even to their own residents, the keepers and hostlers must have looked like mountain men. Or worse. Twain described them as "low, rough characters . . . and from western Nebraska to Nevada a considerable sprinkling of them might be fairly set down as outlaws."[12]

The stations were the lifeblood of a stage and mail line. Without them there could have been no overland service. Ideally, they were situated every twelve to fifteen miles apart, twenty at the most. Unfortunately, the ideal situation was not always the case and was the exception more than the rule through Texas and the Southwest. Thirty, forty, even fifty mile stages without relays were common during the first year of Butterfield's service.

During the long 113 mile stage from Emigrant Crossing on the Pecos River to Pope's Camp, a herd of mules was driven along with Ormsby's stagecoach, but the terribly dry route across the Staked Plains and up the Pecos took its toll on the animals and some had to be left behind. "An enterprising company," he wrote, "is not to be frightened by trivial obstacles, and it will be a matter of economy with them to build stations in preference to killing their stock with such long and arduous drives."[13]

The same held true for the San Antonio-San Diego mail. For either line, Indian raids or lack of sufficient forage left many stations without a fresh or usable team when a coach rolled in. All too frequently, the team that had just come out of harness had to go back in for the opposite bound coach. On several occasions, when two opposite bound stagecoaches heading for the same station were within sight of each other, a race ensued to see which would arrive first and get the fresh team—if there was one.

Not all stations offered meals to the travelers. Most of them were merely swing, or change, stations where only the teams were changed. The larger home, or meal, stations housed anywhere from four to six employees and included the station master, herders, harness maker, cook, and blacksmith. About half that number lived at the change stations except in Indian country where as many as ten men could be found. Passengers and luggage were changed to another coach about every 300 miles.

Drivers began and ended their runs at the home stations, which were situated every forty to fifty miles apart. They would rest up a day or so, then drive the opposite bound coach back over the same route. If a relief driver wasn't available, however, he had to keep going as in the case of Henry Skillman, who drove Waterman Ormsby's coach all the way from the Pecos River to El Paso, some 250 miles. Conductors, those men who rode on the box with the drivers and included horn blowing among their many duties, worked longer stages, usually an entire division.

On the central routes, the second man on the box was an express messenger who was responsible for the strongboxes and express cargo on board. Frank Root worked for the Central Overland and Pikes Peak Express in this capacity. Traveling the Atchison to Denver stretch, he made only $62.50 a month plus his meals on the road. Root said that he often rode on the box for six days and nights without sleep except what he could snatch sitting up.[14]

Western stations along the overland routes differed greatly from those in the more "civilized" areas. There were no Menger or Nimitz Hotels or Camp Inns through the lonely reaches of the Concho River region, Trans-Pecos, or New Mexico and Arizona. More typical was the stage stand in Uvalde, about eighty miles west of San Antonio on the Lower Road. Here Phocian Way stayed the night in the spring of 1858.

"We stopped at a hard-looking tavern," he wrote, "—a stone building with [a] dirt floor, no window glass and canvas for partitions. It was already filled with travelers or boarders—8 or 10 beds in one room. All our party except myself rolled themselves up in their blankets and slept out of doors on the ground. They done better than I, for they slept soundly while I was nearly devoured by the fleas."[15]

Further along, his coach stopped for dinner at a "primitive looking place . . . It is such a house as I never saw before I came to Texas . . . a regular backwood establishment."[16]

One overland traveler described the stations' floors as being "much like the ground outside, only not nearly so clean."[17]

Stations were built with whatever material was available locally. In the east, they were usually log, dog-trot cabins, with a corral nearby. Timber became more scarce as one traveled westward from Fort Chadbourne and adobe, that ages old combination of sun and mud, became the dominant feature. Upon reaching an adobe station on the Pecos River, Albert Richardson wrote, "Thence I traveled eight hundred miles before I again saw a wooden building."[18]

Between Fort Kearney, Nebraska, and Denver, every building was adobe. The roofs were thatched and sodded or covered with a thick layer of earth leading Mark Twain to comment that "It was the first time we had ever seen a man's front yard on top of his house."[19]

Twain said that one had to stoop to enter the front (and only) door. One particular station he described had no window, but only one "square hole about large enough for a man to crawl through . . . There was no flooring, but the ground was packed hard." He also wrote that a fireplace served as stove, and the single room lacked shelves, cupboards, or closets. A single piece of "yellow bar-soap" rested next to the tin wash basin on the ground outside the door. There were no towels, except for a "hoary blue woolen shirt . . ." But, he explained that this was strictly for the station keeper's use; there were none set aside for anyone as inconsequential as passengers. "We had towels," Twain continued, ". . . in the valise; they might as well have been in Sodom and Gomorrah."[20]

The appearance of the stations became more substantial as one traveled westward. Beginning at the Head of Concho Station and throughout Comanche, Kiowa, and Apache territory to Mission Camp in Arizona, some twenty-five Butterfield stations were built fortress-like on the square or rectangular plan similar to the posada, or inn, that was introduced into Mexico by the Spaniards.

The rooms for cooking, sleeping, and storage were attached to the inside walls of the Butterfield stations. At the home stations there would be additional rooms for blacksmith and harness shops, all within the inner compound, the walls of which were two to three feet thick and eleven feet high. Sometimes the mules and horses were penned in this same enclosure; otherwise, an adjoining corral held the stock. An outer wall usually surrounded the entire station.

Westbound passengers could expect no luxuries once they left San Antonio, North Texas, Missouri, or Eastern Kansas. In 1875 an easterner staying at the Menger Hotel in San Antonio had planned to travel to El Paso, "until he heard that at some of the hotels on the road gas was not used in the reading rooms."[21] He would have been even more flabbergasted had he known there weren't any hotels, much less reading rooms, west of Fredericksburg.

Even the "civilized" towns on the eastern portion of the Butterfield line didn't necessarily guarantee the traveler the refinements to which he might be accustomed. Such was the case Albert Richardson found at Springfield, Missouri. He thought the town of 2,500 pleasant enough, but Smith's Tavern, where Overland passengers took their meals and, if they desired, a room, left a lot to be desired.

"The low straggling hotel with high belfry, was on the rural southern model: dining-room full of flies, with a long paper-covered frame swinging to and fro over the table to keep them from the food; the bill of fare, bacon[,] corn bread and coffee; the rooms ill-furnished, towels missing, pitchers empty, and the bed and table linen seeming to have been dragged through the nearest pond, and dried upon grid-irons."[22]

Many of the inns in Eastern Texas in the 1840s were rather primitive themselves. At least, such was Dr. Ferdinand Roemer's impression during his travels. At a "tavern" in Seguin, he found four large beds in the sleeping quarters; but since there were twice as many bodies as there were beds, ". . . it was self-evident that each bed would be occupied by two persons."[23]

In New Braunfels, where he spent another night, the sleeping conditions were particularly miserable even though the house itself was a "large, stately manor" and the proprietor was friendly and obliging. For the travelers' comfort, mattresses had been spread on the floor in the attic. Roemer managed to capture a small one for his use and spread a thin cotton blanket over himself, when the host assigned a stranger to share his bed. The author spent the night battling for his half of the blanket.[24]

The North Texas town of Sherman was proud of its Butterfield station. A reporter for the local paper described the structure in 1859 as the "most imposing public institution in Sherman, not of course the handsomest building, but large with wide doors always open and having a look of night and day work unceasing which makes one think of public establishments in old cities."[25]

The stations along both the Butterfield and San Antonio-San Diego routes were named for obvious local landmarks, usually for the springs or rivers where they were located. Idaho stations were named "with sardonic humor" according to their location. "One is called Forest Grove," wrote Albert Richardson, "because there is not a single tree within fifteen miles; another, Cold Spring, because not a drop of water exists in the vicinity."[26]

The postwar stand at the temporarily abandoned Fort Stockton in West Texas took on a more personal moniker. When beans seemed to be the only repast available to travelers and workers alike, it became known as "Beans Station." A larger variety of foods later became available when William Russell set up a stand and advertised that travelers on the San Antonio-El Paso road could be supplied with "corn, flour, and beans at Comanche [Springs] or Fort Stockton."[27]

John Butterfield's men in charge of building stations along the 2,700 mile route were fortunate enough to find some existing structures ready to occupy. Fort Phantom Hill was one, ". . . the cheapest and best new station on the route," as Ormsby described it. He was particularly impressed with the station keeper, Mr. Burlington, and his wife who were ". . . all alone, hundreds of miles from any settlement . . . fearless of the attacks of blood-thirsty Indians—as brave a man as ever settled on a frontier . . . ."[28]

Pope's Camp Station was another of the ready real estate sites and was undoubtedly the most unusual station in the Southwest. This fortress-like camp, the only collection of permanent buildings between Fort Chadbourne and El Paso, had been built by Captain John Pope in the spring of 1855 during his water well exploration and was abandoned in July of 1858, just in time for the mail company to inhabit.

The site, just south of the present Texas and New Mexico border, was strategically located on the highest prominence in the area about three hundred feet from the Pecos River and near a good spring. The buildings were constructed of stone and adobe and the enclosing wall was laid out in the form of an irregular five-pointed star. Many of the buildings within the wall were connected by cobblestone walkways and had stone paved floors, large fireplaces, and even porches, which were also paved with limestone slabs. As impressive as it already was, the place must have seemed like heaven to those early Butterfield passengers.[29]

Another well-placed station on the Southern Overland route was the Pinery, sixty-four miles west of Pope's Camp. Situated at the summit of treacherous Guadalupe Mountains Pass, this meal and change station hugged the eastern flank of the mountain range which Ormsby could see so clearly in the moonlight from the Pecos River. The Pinery, at more than 5,600 feet in elevation, was the highest Butterfield stand on the original route. Only the corral had been completed when Ormsby stopped here on the evening of September 28, 1858, twelve days out of St. Louis, and the station keepers and construction men were living in tents.[30]

Water from the spring, located a quarter of a mile up from the station in a grove of cool pine trees, flowed downhill through a ditch to a tank situated within the thirty-inch thick walls. Henry Ramstein was the agent here during the station's brief career and he had six to eight helpers, including herders, a smithy, and a cook. Like most overland stands, the Pinery was busier than one might imagine in spite of its remoteness. In addition to the arrivals of the coaches four times a week, emigrant trains, freighters, and express riders came through frequently. Company tank wagons also stopped to take on water to carry to less favorably endowed stations on the route.[28]

By far the largest station on the Butterfield route, or possibly any other, was the one at El Paso. Built by Anson Mills and completed the month of the inaugural runs, it covered some two acres, bounded 141 feet on the north by Overland Street, and 112 feet on the east and west by Oregon Street and El Paso Street, respectively. The main adobe building resembled a Mexican style ranch house and occupied close to half a city block, a facade facing El Paso Street included an arcade with ten arches. Several 14-by-16 foot rooms enclosed the 43-by-72 foot courtyard. The walls were twenty feet high and nearly three feet thick.[32]

Some stations were privately owned ranch or farm houses, their owners becoming Butterfield employees to supplement their usually meager incomes. Such a station was Franz's, twenty-two miles southwest of Fort Belknap. James Madison Franz built his one-story log home around 1856 or 1857. In 1858 it became a meal station on the Overland. The house had two rooms, one of which was the family's own quarters and doubled as parlor and bedroom. The other room was for the benefit of the station and it served as sleeping and dining rooms and kitchen.

The stock tenders slept in the stable and ate with the family. The Franz's daughter, Elizabeth Francis, was about twelve years old when the Butterfield operation began. She recalled the arrivals and departures of the coaches and her mother cooking meals over the open fireplace for the passengers and station helpers. Sometimes everyone had to get up in the middle of the night to prepare for an incoming stagecoach and her mother wouldn't allow anyone to go back to bed until all the dishes had been washed.[33]

The Civil War had an impact on the nature and quality of some stage stops, at least according to H. H. McConnell, who was stationed at Fort Richardson in the late 1860s. Like many soldiers garrisoned at the frontier posts, he frequently traveled by stagecoach and was impressed by the rest stops between

San Antonio and Jack County. "Just about those days in Texas," he wrote, "I think there were some of the best country stage-stands or wayside hotels in the world."[34]

Many, he explained, were owned by Texans who had been displaced or financially ruined by the war, especially women widowed during the conflict. Suddenly thrown upon their own initiatives, they opened up hotels or inns along the heavily traveled roads. ". . . the result was," McConnell wrote, "the best stopping places imaginable. The fact is, the unequaled broiled or 'smothered' chicken, the hot biscuits, the fragrant coffee (it takes a Southern woman to make this just right), are . . . 'the brightest spots in memory's waste.'"[35]

When Ben Ficklin took over most of the staging business throughout West Texas after the war, he either built new stations or remodeled existing Butterfield structures. A hundred years later, with the old stagecoach stations in ruins, it is often easy to tell one from the other by the foundations.

The Butterfield company built their stations with the dwellings and storage structures attached to the inside walls. Ficklin moved them outside, usually one on each side of the entrance. James Gillett, the Texas Ranger, described the Ficklin stands with good detail.

"On each side of the entrance was a large room. The gateway opened into a passageway, which was roofed and extended from one room to the other. In the rear of the rooms was the corral, the walls of which were six to eight feet high and two feet thick, also of sun-dried brick. One room was used for cooking and eating and the other for sleeping quarters and storage."[36]

Ficklin became such an entrepreneur in the business that his headquarters, built on the Middle Concho River near San Angelo, grew into a thriving community that became the seat of Tom Green County. H. G. Logan, the traveling correspondent of the San Antonio *Herald*, described Benficklin, the town, in 1873 as "a beautiful little village . . . containing some twelve or fifteen buildings for animals and good storage shelter."[37] The town remained the county seat from January of 1875 to

August of 1882, when a flood on the 24th washed everything down the Concho.

Arrivals at stations supplied much of the mystique of the stagecoach era. Trains had their wailing whistles to signal their approach to town; the white sails of the schooners could be seen while they were yet miles at sea. But the stagecoach had the post horn.

"The blast of the stage horn," wrote an overland passenger in 1859, "as it rolls through the valleys and over the prairies of the West, cheers and gladdens the heart of the pioneer . . . He knows that it brings tidings from the hearts and homes he left behind him . . . ."[38]

The post horn had a long history of tradition on the post roads dating from its use in England and the early roads of the Atlantic states. The horn that was used in the West was a brass bugle introduced to western staging by John Butterfield. It had evolved from the long, slender and curved *waldhorn*, or hunting horn, and later from the orchestral French horn.

"Throughout our Overland journey," wrote Tallack, "our approach to a station, whether previous to a relay or a meal, was announced at a distance by a long blast from the conductor's horn, often heard far away in the silence of the wilds . . . ."[39]

Romantic as it was, the horn's use on the mail roads had a more practical purpose. Heard from a distance of a half mile or more, a blast from the horn gave the station personnel time to hitch a fresh team and warm up the beans and coffee.

For town residents, the arrival of a stagecoach was as much an observance as a Saturday night dance. The coach brought mail, newspapers from as far away as New York or San Francisco, maybe even a new resident. Lonely men in mining towns were anxious to see if any new "ladies" were aboard to liven up the local saloons. Whenever the residents of Salado, in Bell County, Texas, heard the horn, everyone would rush to the hotel where any literate citizen who subscribed to an eastern newspaper was expected to read aloud to the crowd the important news stories.[40]

During the 1850s the citizens of Round Rock, Texas, north of Austin, had two ways of knowing when a stagecoach was coming. Every time the post horn was sounded, the large flock of geese kept at the Harris Stagecoach Inn to supply feathers for the hotel's pillows and mattresses would begin honking and kept up their cacophony until the coach had arrived.[41]

Nowhere was an arrival any more welcome that to those "inmates" of the distant stage stations. Albert Richardson learned firsthand how important the stagecoach was to the men and women at the secluded stands. "One night," he wrote, "when we rolled up to a lonely station, miles from any other human habitation, the stock-tender, ragged, shaggy, sunburned and unkempt, put his lantern up to our coach window and implored: 'Gentlemen, can you spare me a newspaper? I have not seen one for a week and can't endure it much longer.'" Richardson said the man was willing to pay a dollar for any U.S. paper not older than ten days.[42]

Perhaps no one wrote of a stagecoach's arrival with more enthusiasm than did a resident of Fort Belknap upon the arrival of the first Butterfield coach on September 22, 1858. ". . . bring out your big gun, rooster, or anything that will make a big noise. Next to the Atlantic cable this is the greatest triumph of the present day . . . ."[43]

Notes, Chapter Eight

1. William A. Duffen, Ed., "Overland Via 'Jackass Mail' in 1858. The Diary of Phocion R. Way," *Arizona and the West*, 2:1, 43.
2. William Tallack, *The California Overland Express. The Longest Stage-Ride in the West*, 48.
3. Albert D. Richardson, *Beyond the Mississippi: From the Great River to the Great Ocean*, 232-233.
4. William Banning and George Hugh Banning, *Six Horses*, 150-151.
5. Roscoe P. Conkling and Margaret B. Conkling, *The Butterfield Overland Mail, 1857-1869*, I: 349.
6. Ibid., ii: 36-38. The three volumes of the authors are considered the source for not only tracing the Butterfield mail route in its entire length, but also for extensive research on all of the station ruins found. Historians interested in the route are indebted to the Conklings for their personal studies of the stations, many of which are no longer discernible or available to the public.
7. Col. Nathaniel Alston Taylor, *The Coming Empire, or, Two Thousand Miles in Texas on Horseback*, 357.
8. Richardson, 234.
9. Travelers still find Hueco Tanks, now a state park, a fascinating place to stop.
10. Frank A. Root and William Elsey Connelley, *The Overland Stage to California*, 67.
11. Richardson, 340.
12. Mark Twain, *Roughing It*, 27.
13. Waterman L. Ormsby, *The Butterfield Overland Mail*, 91-92. Ormsby listed the longest stages without team changes, all but three being in Texas: Fort Chadbourne to Grape Creek, 30 miles; Grape Creek to Head of the Concho, 50 miles; Head of the Concho to Pecos River, 75 miles; Pecos River to Pope's Camp, 113 miles; Pope's Camp to Guadalupe Mountains (the Pinery), 60 miles; Guadalupe Pass to Cornudas, 60 miles; Picacho (Arizona) to Cooke's Spring, 52 miles; Mimbres River to Soldier's Farewell, 50 miles; and Soldier's Farewell to Stein's Peak, 42 miles.
14. Root and Connelley, 73, 79
15. Duffen, 2:1, 43.
16. Ibid.

17. Wayne Gard, et al., *Along the Early Trails of the Southwest*, 33.
18. Richardson, 233.
19. Twain, 16.
20. Ibid.
21. San Antonio *Daily Herald*, 21 August 1875.
22. Richardson, 207-208.
23. Dr. Ferdinand Roemer, *Texas*, 293.
24. Ibid., 297-298.
25. Sherman *Democrat*, 3 August 1947.
26. Richardson, 504.
27. San Antonio *Daily Herald*, 21 April 1867, and 12 May 1867.
28. Ormsby, 50. The fort was officially designated as the "Post on the Clear Fork of the Brazos" and was said to have gained the name Phantom Hill from the ghostly appearance of its chimneys in the moonlight.
29. Conkling and Conkling, I: 379. The camp also became a prominent stop on the Goodnight-Loving cattle trail. Unfortunately, the site was destroyed when Red Bluff Reservoir was created on this stretch of the Pecos River.
30. Ormsby, 73-74; Conkling and Conkling, I: 390-393. The station was abandoned the following August when the upper route was abandoned. Today, the ruins of the Pinery Station are located about two hundred feet off of U.S. Highway 62/180, and are part of the Guadalupe Mountains National Park.
31. Dava McGahee Davy, "The Pinery Station." No page number.
32. Conkling and Conkling, II: 59-61.
33. Ibid., I: 320-321.
34. H. H. McConnell, *Five Years A Cavalryman*, 190.
35. Ibid., 190-191.
36. James B. Gillett, *Six Years With the Texas Rangers, 1875 to 1881*, 146-147.
37. San Antonio *Daily Herald*, 17 September 1873.
38. San Francisco *Bulletin*, 13 June 1859. In LeRoy R. Hafen, *The Overland Mail*, 99.
39. Tallack, 49-50.
40. Kathryn Turner Carter, *Stagecoach Inns of Texas*, 189.
41. Ibid., 176.
42. Richardson, 331.
43. Barbara A. Neal Ledbetter, *Fort Belknap*, 77.

CHAPTER NINE
"By their courage the west was made"

" . . . the driver was the only
being they bowed down to and
worshipped."[1]

"We wish those who oppose railroads had been with us this morning, and listened to a sorrel-topped stage driver play the violin . . . ."[2]

This piece, which appeared in the San Antonio *Daily Herald* in August of 1875, about a driver who was practicing the instrument in the backyard of the stage office, went on to say that the noise "destroyed the appetite of boarders at the Menger Hotel, a hundred yards distant."[3]

So what if he couldn't play a violin; chances are he could corner a smoking six-in-hand as deftly as any musician ever pulled a bow over the strings. And what violinist could perform so many feats simultaneously as did the driver of a particular stagecoach bound for the California gold fields? As a passenger on the vehicle observed:

"He drove little Spanish mules to the stage, two at the wheels and three as leaders, he carried a shotgun and two six shooters. He kept his head turning in all directions all the time, managing to pull the reins, flourish his whip, keep his mules in a gallop, hold a finger on the trigger of three firearms, and talk all at the same time . . . ."[4]

Our sorrel-topped stage driver notwithstanding, many Jehus were capable musicians. "Quite a number could play different musical instruments," wrote Frank Root. "The violin was the favorite with most of them." Root went on to say that the banjo and guitar and even such instruments as one would not expect from members of their profession as the clarinet, flute, and piccolo. Root said further that one driver could "rip a five-octave jew's harp all to pieces."[5]

No doubt about it, the American stagecoach driver was a special breed of man, as epic in size and importance to his time and place as was the cowboy to his. Visitors from England were quick to notice the difference between their own drivers and those of the former Colonies, even down to their attire. James Silk Buckingham, who traveled through the states in the 1840s, wrote that the American driver was, for the most part, "very ill-dressed, though civil and well qualified for his duty."[6]

Jim Spears, standing at right in front of the new Ben Ficklin (Benficklin) jail in 1878, drove stagecoaches for the man for whom the town was named and was also sheriff. (Courtesy Fort Concho National Historic Landmark)

Hank Monk, bundled head to toe for the bitter cold on his route over the Sierras, is not wearing gloves. Like many true reinsmen, he disdained the use of heavy gloves because they did not allow him to "feel" the reins in his hands. (Courtesy of Wells Fargo Bank History Room)

PICTURE MADE AT CONCHO MAIL STATION, 1879, TOM GREEN COUNTY, TEXAS. DRIVER: ELISHA BATES, GENERAL SUPT. STAGE STATION. FRONT SEAT: FRANCIS C. TAYLOR. LITTLE GIRL IN COACH: ADA CLAPP, DAUGHTER OF MR. CLAPP, BLACKSMITH AND PAINTER FOR STATION.

A six-horse team hitched to a Celerity wagon at Concho mail station. Notice the 'rumble seat' at rear of coach. (Courtesy Fort Concho National Historic Landmark)

East Texas drivers seemed to have maintained a "civilized look" about their dress. At least, Ferdinand Roemer thought so during his travels through the young state. "He presented an unmistakable specimen of his nation as well as his trade, in his neat suit and white shirt sleeves and also in the safety with which he handled his four black mules . . . ."[7]

The English stagecoach driver seemed more a servant than the absolute "captain of the ship" that was his American counterpart. For one, American drivers, sometimes called "whips" or "Jehus," accepted no tips from the passengers. Of course, they weren't above accepting a proffered cigar or swig from a parting passenger's flask on a cold day.

Many travelers, however, might have preferred giving the driver a little something in return for good service. An English traveler in the 1830s found it lacking on the eastern post roads. "As the driver never expects or demands a fee from the passengers," he wrote, "they or their comforts are no concern of his . . . ."[8]

John Butterfield made it clear that his employees ". . . are expected to show proper respect to and treat passengers and the public with civility . . . ."[9]

By most accounts, his drivers considered the rules gospel, as did the majority of others. A passenger who rode a Butterfield stagecoach from San Francisco to Yuma, Arizona, in October of 1858, praised the men on the box. "The drivers employed by the Company are not only the best 'whips' I have ever seen, but the most cheerful, happy and polite set of men to be met with anywhere."[10]

Waterman Ormsby was another who found the Overland employees "without exception, to be courteous, civil, and attentive." Ormsby tempered his enthusiasm a bit saying that a few "are a little reckless and too anxious to make fast time, but as a general thing they are very cautious."[11]

Throughout Western staging, drivers came with so many backgrounds and personalities that it would seem impossible to characterize them as a whole. But a few contemporary travelers and writers were able to present a general picture.

W. W. Mills, who lived in El Paso during the heyday of stagecoaching in the West, found their character "difficult to describe .... He possessed the courage of the soldier and something more, the stage driver in those times had to be as alert and thoughtful as a General." To Mills, the drivers' duties and responsibilities to the company, the government mails, and his passengers, were what set him above others of his time. "Like the sailor, he was something of a fatalist, but he believed in using all possible means to protect himself and those under his charge."[12]

Mills found them to be rather shy and reluctant to talk about themselves. "When, however, he could be induced to talk about himself as a stage driver, his stories were always interesting and sometimes thrilling. There was occasionally a liar among them, but most of them had really experienced such serious adventures and 'hair-breadth scapes' that it was not necessary for them to draw upon their imaginations."[13]

Mark Twain, however, found some drivers who weren't above stretching the truth a bit. One of the coaches he rode in had a hole through the front, the result of an earlier Indian attack. The driver was wounded in that confrontation, but "he did not mind it much," Twain wrote. "He said the place to keep a man 'huffy' was down on the southern Overland, among the Apaches, before the company moved the stage line up the northern [central] route. He said the Apaches used to annoy him all the time down there, and that he came as near as anything to starving to death in the midst of abundance, because they kept him so leaky with bullet-holes that he 'couldn't hold his vittles'." Twain was not impressed; he said the man could not be believed.[14]

As one might imagine, their language at times could make the proverbial fish-wife shrink. Yet, however rough and profane a driver was around other men, Mills found them to be "remarkably courteous to lady passengers and ever thoughtful of their comfort and feelings, and more than once, on arriving at a station where the drivers were to be changed, I have heard one whisper to another: 'Remember, Sandy, there is a little lady in the coach.' This was sufficient."[15]

Albert Richardson recalled one of his experiences wherein the driver, despite the presence of a preacher sitting next to him, swore "long and loud" at the team.

"'My friend'," began the preacher, "'don't swear so. Remember Job; he was severely tried, but never lost his patience.'

"'Job—Job?'," the driver countered. "'What line did *he* drive for?'"[16]

Upon describing the hierarchy of Overland employees, Mark Twain said that next to the Division Superintendent in rank and importance was the conductor. Yet he was treated "merely with the best of what was their idea of civility, but the *driver* was the only being they bowed down to and worshipped. How admiringly they would gaze up at him in his high seat as he gloved himself with lingering deliberation, while some happy hostler held the bunch of reins aloft, and waited patiently for him to take it!"[17]

The driver was, admittedly, Twain's "delight." With their shifts ending each day or night, ". . . we never got as well acquainted with them as we did with the conductors; and besides, they would have been above being familiar with such rubbish as passengers, anyhow . . . . Still, we were always eager to get a sight of each and every new driver as soon as the watch changed, for . . . we were either anxious to get rid of an unpleasant one, or loath to part with a driver we had learned to like . . . ."[18]

At each station, Twain observed a ritual peculiar to the profession and the men's reputation for showmanship. While the teams were being changed, the driver would toss the gathered reins to the ground, stretch complacently, then pull off his fine buckskin gloves, always "with great deliberation and insufferable dignity—taking not the slightest notice of a dozen solicitous inquiries after his health . . . from five or six hairy and half-civilized station-keepers and hostlers . . . for in the eyes of the stage-driver of that day, station-keepers and hostlers were a sort of good enough low creatures, useful in their place . . . but not the kind of beings which a person of distinction could afford to concern himself with; while on the contrary, in the eyes of the station-keeper and the hostler, the stage-driver was a hero—a great and shining dignitary, the world's favorite son.... When they spoke to him they received his insolent silence meekly, and as being the natural and proper conduct of so great a man; when he opened his lips they all hung on his words with admiration; when he discharged a facetious insulting personality at a hostler, that hostler was happy for the day.... And how they would fly around when he wanted a basin of water ... or a light for his pipe!"[19]

But Twain added that if a passenger dared to request such favors, the result could be humiliating. "... for let it be borne in mind, the Overland driver had but little less contempt for his passengers than he had for his hostlers."[20]

The importance and awe with which drivers were held by other company employees is evidenced by an incident that occurred in 1868 on a central route. A coach carrying Speaker of the House—and future vice president under President Grant—Schuyler Colfax arrived at a station well after midnight. Colfax hinted that he was hungry, but the station keeper's sleepy wife seemed reluctant to start a meal at this hour. But when the driver mentioned that he could use something to eat, the lady's attitude changed quickly and, as a traveling companion of Colfax reported, "breakfast for all [was] forthcoming."[21]

J. Ross Browne was not a big admirer of the Jehus. "Why stage-drivers, who are paid a liberal stipend per month for putting passengers over the public highways," he once remarked, "should be so vindictively hostile to the travelling community surpasses my comprehension."[22]

Considering the hours that they often had to work at a stretch, it is not surprising that stagecoach drivers were less than hospitable at times. Even though they were supposed to drive certain distances before being relieved, circumstances often arose when working double shifts was necessary. Sometimes he had to take the reins of the opposite bound coach and would be back on the box before having time to catch more than a short nap.

One driver of Twain's coach was doing double duty. He had already driven seventy-five miles and was having to drive the return shift without benefit of a rest. Twain was flabbergasted. "A hundred and fifty miles of holding back six vindictive mules and keeping them from climbing the trees!"[23]

In such cases, they often slept on the box. When Twain discovered that a driver of his coach was sound asleep with the mules running at breakneck speed through the Rocky Mountains, the conductor assured him that there was no danger. ". . . a sleeping man *will* seize the irons in time when the coach jolts," Twain was assured.[24]

The driver of the stagecoach in Nevada one night in 1865 was not so lucky. The only person on the box, he had fallen asleep, tumbled overboard, and was crushed by the wheels. The coach made it three miles to the station on its own, with its only two passengers, a woman and a child, unaware of the tragedy.[25]

The most coveted seat on a coach was the one next to the driver and he alone had the final say on who occupied it. Maybe the honor went to a VIP, or a journalist. But, if a young and pretty and single lady were on board, no one else stood a ghost of a chance.

Oscar Winther hinted that a passenger desiring to sit with the driver had to go about it in much the same manner as if he were "securing an appointment to a high office;" that is, perhaps he should go over the driver's head, to the president of the company himself. But, woe betide the pushy passenger, for he was likely to incur such wrath and ill treatment from his Jehu that he wished he had stayed home.[26]

An Englishman traveling through the American West, took the driver's status a step further and wrote that he "is inferior to no one in the Republic. Even the President, were he on board, must submit to his higher authority."[27]

Some boys wanted to be stage drivers as fervently as others longed to be cowboys or sailors, and those who did began practicing when they were seven or eight years old, devoting several hours a day to practicing the art. A youngster with such ambitions was especially fortunate if his father was a reinsman. It took several years to become accomplished enough to graduate to a Concord coach with a team of six spirited horses. By the time the boy was seventeen or eighteen, if he had learned his lessons well, his father would give him his very own custom-made whip. A boy who aspired to that profession could receive no greater a reward.[28]

John J. Reynolds was one who practiced diligently when he was a tad, and he used an unusual method to learn the art. He would poke half a dozen sticks into the ground in the same manner that a team would be positioned and harnessed, tie strings to each, and hold the lines as he would the reins of a span of six. The goal was to dislodge any of the sticks with just a slight movement of a finger or fingers without disturbing the others. Reynolds went on to become the highest paid reinsman in California. "John Reynolds," wrote the Bannings, ". . . when it came to six real lines and six real horses, could work this telegraphy to perfection."[29]

In a six-horse team, each span was referred to, from front to rear, as leaders, swings, and wheelers. A four-horse hitch consisted only of the leaders and wheelers. Off meant the right side; near, or nigh, the left. The off leader was the right-hand leader from the driver's box.

Fiction writers and movie makers overdo the use of the whip. Banning said it was bad practice to start the team with the lash. The whip, a hickory stock five feet long with an eleven or twelve foot buckskin lash, was held in the right hand with the butt resting in the palm and the stock held parallel to the lines. It was used mainly for intimidating the wheelers, the slowest members of the span. Banning said that it wasn't long enough to reach the leaders of a six-horse team, but there were a few drivers who used a twenty-two foot lash.[30]

A driver's whip was a very personal thing to him and he would have it engraved or embossed with silver or lead. It was an extension of himself and his personality and was therefore governed by a set of taboos, including never wrapping the thongs around the stock or allowing a whip out of its owner's sight. Drivers didn't lend them even to their most trusted friends.

While some drivers boasted that they could pop a fly off the back of the nigh leader with a flick of the whip without turning a hair on the animal, others bragged that they rarely needed to use one. Banning called the latter reinsmen and he explained the difference. A reinsman "was a master driver who, by virtue of his exceptional skill, was able to drive each span of his complement wholly independent of the other. It was a happy team whose driver was a reinsman."[31]

In a six-horse hitch, the reins, or ribbons, in a driver's hands resembled a hopeless tangle to the uninitiated. But each strand had its place. The reins for the leaders were held between the index and middle fingers of each hand; those for the swings, between the middle and third fingers; and those for the wheelers, between the third and little fingers. Amidst the jumble of leather in the right hand, the whip was grasped between the thumb and forefinger with the butt secured against the heel of the thumb. The reins were played through the fingers, gathering each line by drawing with the fingers on each side and letting them out by separating the fingers just enough to let the ribbon slip. A top driver sat with his hands resting in his lap and a passenger sitting next to him was hard pressed to see any movement in the man's fingers.

It was because of this need to "feel" the reins that these drivers never wore heavy gloves. If gloves were worn at all, they were silk or the finest buckskin, even in the bitterest of cold. Many drivers lost fingers to frostbite.

Turning, or cornering, a coach was a marvel to witness with a true reinsman on the box. Approaching a turn, and while still some hundred yards distant, the driver would move his right foot to rest ever so lightly on the pedal of the brake shaft. At the moment the turn was to be initiated, he would barely press the brake handle. An experienced team knew the sound and pricked their ears in anticipation of the change in direction. Good coach horses also knew their own names and understood the driver's tone of voice. Making a sharp turn, then, was a clever combination of reining, slight braking, and voice.

A first-class reinsman preferred a loosely hitched team to one that was so tightly harnessed that the animals had to move as a single unit. A loosely hitched span performed individually and a top driver could hold the wheelers steady while the leaders made the turn.

Hank Monk was a driver who took this art to the peak of perfection. It was said that he could make a U-turn in the middle of a street with his six-in-hand at a full gallop and all reins loose. This was an object, it must be remembered, that was some fifty feet long from the leaders' noses to the Concord's rear wheels.[32]

While Banning described good driving as poetry in motion and pictured an elegant, well-cared-for Concord with a "happy" span of six, neither poetry in motion, nor a "happy" span of any kind were the realities of staging over the Southwest. In the first place, mules were never happy with what they were doing, and the last place they wanted to be was in harness. It often took nothing less than brute force to manage them. Here, too, the whip was exercised more freely, although its overuse was still considered detrimental.

An excellent cross-country time for a stagecoach was considered to be 150 miles a day, or just over six miles per hour. Ten miles an hour over good, flat roads was "bragging time" and anything over that was just plain foolish.

A British traveler concluded from his journeys throughout California that Western stage drivers were daring and reckless and were of the opinion that the only way to go down mountain roads was "to rush it."[33]

Waterman Ormsby would have agreed following one of his own experiences. If he were a religious man he probably recalled the Biblical passage from 2 Kings, 9:20: "... and the driving is like the driving of Jehu ... for he driveth furiously."

From Ormsby's description, California's Pacheco Pass must have been the most alarming stretch of road on the Butterfield route. For twelve miles, the road hugged sheer cliffs that dropped off to seemingly bottomless voids. One would think it required cautious driving. At least Ormsby thought so. "But our Jehu was in a hurry with the 'first States' mail'" he wrote, "and he was bound to put us through in good time." When Ormsby, who was riding on the box, suggested that one could depart this life at any moment should anything break, the driver assured him that nothing would, whereupon he "whipped up his horses just as we started down a steep hill."[34]

Ormsby at least expected to see the driver keep his foot on the brake bar during the ascent, but the latter told him it was best to "'keep the wheels rolling, or they'll slide' . . . so he did keep the wheels rolling, and the whole coach slid down the steepest hills at the rate of fifteen—yes, twenty—miles an hour, now turning an abrupt curve with a whip and crack and 'round the corner, Sally' . . . . We flew at a rate I know would have made old John Butterfield . . . a very experienced stage man, wish himself safely at home."[35]

Another rider who may have wished himself safely at home was Horace Greeley when fate put him in a stagecoach driven by Hank Monk. Henry James Monk was one of the better known drivers in California, famed for his expertise with the reins. Greeley, the outspoken founder and editor of the New York *Tribune*, had headed west to California in 1860. On this particular day, he boarded Monk's coach for the downhill run over the Sierras to Placerville, where he was scheduled to lecture. Greeley made the mistake of asking Monk for quick time lest he be late. That was all a Jehu with Monk's capabilities and ego needed. He urged the team into a run and gravity did the rest. Soon they were careening down the mountain and around the turns at such a rate that Greeley could not keep his seat, or his composure. When he called out that he wasn't in *that* big a hurry, Monk replied, "Keep your seat, Horace, I'll get you there on time!"[36]

The day after that wild ride, Monk awarded Greeley the ultimate honor on the latter's return trip—a place next to him on the box. Greeley himself never forgot the experience and said later that Monk was "the only man ever to make me look the fool."[37]

Stage drivers particularly liked to show their skills upon arrival in towns where there was certain to be a crowd. On this note Albert Richardson observed that the driver would urge his team to its fastest and enter town at a full gallop. As the hotel was neared, he would begin applying the brake and eventually bring his team to a clean stop on a dime at the hotel's steps.

The arrival of the first Butterfield mail coach in San Francisco on the Sunday morning of October 10, 1858, did so with just such flair. "Soon we struck the pavements," Ormsby wrote, "and with a whip, crack, and bound, shot through the streets to our destination, to the great consternation of everything in the way . . . Swiftly we whirled up one street and down another, and round the corners, until finally we drew up at the stage office in front of the Plaza . . . ."[38]

Drivers were paid well, although not as liberally as one would assume compared with some other employees. On the Central Overland route, the pay scale for Jehus was from $40 to $75 a month, plus board, while harness-makers, blacksmiths, and division agents received up to $125. In the late 1860s, when the Indian problem had reached epidemic proportions, the latter were paid $200 a month and even then were hard to come by.[39]

Capable of holding their own in any bar, drivers usually did not drink while driving; but, there were exceptions. Future president of the United States James A. Garfield journeyed to Montana in 1872 and wrote that the level of genius in one of his Jehus ". . . is exhibited in the ratio of his intoxication" and added that he was a "brilliant" driver.[40]

Sometimes drivers found themselves in embarrassing and touchy situations, particularly if they had a weakness for gambling. Such an instance occurred at Langtry, a rough little town in Southwest Texas on the Rio Grande. The driver of a local stage line was cheated by three gamblers and put up the company's mules and only coach to cover both his losses and one more bet. Again he was bamboozled by the slicks and

Vinegaroon lost its mail service. An angry owner brought the gamblers before Judge Roy Bean's irregular court on the charge of interfering with a public conveyance. Luckily for Langtry's residents, the colorful judge ruled in the mail company's favor and ordered the transgressors to return coach, team, and money. No mention if the driver was relieved of his duties.[41]

John Butterfield picked most of his drivers himself from the Eastern stage roads. Many Western "whips" usually did not follow the painstaking manner of learning their trade in boyhood as did their Eastern counterparts. Many found their way to the driver's box from a variety of backgrounds.

Henry Skillman certainly looked the part of the Western stage driver. Waterman Ormsby thought that he fairly resembled portraits of the Wandering Jew. The expatriated Kentuckian was more than six feet tall, had long yellow hair and beard, wore buckskin, and was heavily adorned with revolvers and Bowie knives. He already had a good deal of staging experience, namely on the San Antonio-El Paso and Santa Fe routes, when he went to work for Butterfield in 1858 at the age of forty-five. When civil war erupted, he joined the Confederacy and was killed in a shootout near Presidio in 1864.[42]

William ("Big Foot") Wallace was another who would have been cast as a stagecoach driver in any movie. Six foot two, and tipping the scales at 240 in his prime, the Virginian of Scottish descent came to Texas at age twenty shortly after the battle at San Jacinto. He worked in every capacity on the frontier, including, Texas Ranger, mail carrier, driver, and rancher.[43]

Henry Daly, a stage driver who had more than his share of 'hair-breadth scapes,' was an eighteen-year-old when he drifted into San Antonio in the late 1860s. First he tried breaking horses then went to work for Ben Ficklin's stage line, ". . . thinking it afforded superior opportunities for excitement and romance."[44]

California driver Charlie Parkhurst was typical of the Western mold. Charlie could drive as well as anyone; curse with the best of them; hold his own with the bottle or cards, although neither to excess; and could always be seen with a stogie or a wad of tobacco in his mouth. During his thirty years on the box, Charlie fought off Indians and bandits, lost an eye from a horse's kick, and developed the driver's plague, rheumatism. Charlie finally retired to a farm near Watsonville, California, and died there of cancer in 1879. One can only imagine the surprise his friends and fellow whips felt when, preparing the body for burial, they discovered that Charlie Parkhurst was a woman!

Most drivers would not have traded their profession with any other and, for the most part, were fiercely loyal to their company. The drivers for Ben Holladay (Chapter Ten) were no different. A Mister Stein, who worked for Holladay, was called the poet of the stage line by many. He wrote a song which appeared in the Montana *Post* on April 8, 1865, was sung fervently by Holladay's drivers, and would have served any driver on any other line. A couple of verses went thusly:

> *"I sing to everybody, in the country and the town,*
> *A song upon a subject that's worthy of renown;*
> *I haven't got a story of fairy-land to broach,*
> *But plead for the cause of sticking to the box seat of a coach.*
> *Statesmen and warriors, traders and the rest,*
> *May boast of their profession, and think it is the best;*
> *Their state I'll never envy, I'll have you understand,*
> *Long as I can be a driver on the jolly 'Overland'."*[45]

Then, as even now, the stagecoach driver of the American West was a hero in the eyes of many, a real legend in his own time and for all time.

One of the drivers' biggest champions was the Texas Ranger Jim Gillett, who wrote:

"There should be a monument erected to the memory of those old stage-drivers somewhere along this overland route, for they were certainly the bravest of the brave. It took a man with lots of nerve and strength to be a stage-driver in the Indian days, and many of them were killed. The very last year the stage line was kept up (1880), several drivers were killed between Fort Davis and El Paso."[46]

Gillett would be happy about the marker that lies embedded in rock at an old watering stop west of Fort Davis. It isn't as large as it should be, and you have to look for it, but it does honor those men that Gillett talked about and maybe says it all.

"Dedicated to the memory of Ed Waldy, John M. Dean, August Frensell and all other stage drivers who traveled this route. Fearless heroes of frontier days. By their courage the west was made."

Notes, Chapter Nine

1. Mark Twain, *Roughing It*, 15.
2. San Antonio *Daily Herald*, 21 August 1875.
3. Ibid.
4. Sherman *Democrat*, 3 August 1947. This five-mule Mexican hitch was not commonly used on American stagecoaches.
5. Frank A. Root and William Elsey Connelley, *The Overland Stage to California*, 268.
6. James S. Buckingham, "The Slave States of America," 1: 234. In Holmes and Rohrbach, *Stagecoach East*, 62-63.
7. Dr. Ferdinand Roemer, *Texas*, 292.
8. Frederick Marryat, "A Diary in America," 2:165. In Holmes and Rohrbach, 61.
9. "Special Instructions."
10. William Tallack, *The California Overland Express*, 73.
11. Waterman L. Ormsby, *The Butterfield Overland Mail*, 94.
12. W. W. Mills, *Forty Years at El Paso. 1858-1898*, 125.
13. Ibid., 126.
14. Twain, 39-40.
15. Mills, 126.
16. Albert D. Richardson, *Beyond the Mississippi: From the Great River to the Great Ocean*, 484.
17. Twain, 15.
18. Ibid., 26.
19. Ibid., 14-15.
20. Ibid.
21. David Nevin, *The Expressmen*, 174.
22. Oscar Osburn Winther, *Via Western Express & Stagecoach*, 61.
23. Twain, 26-27.
24. Ibid., 9.
25. Richardson, 366.
26. Winther, 61.
27. "Half Hours in the Wide West," 144. Reprinted in Atchison *Daily Globe*, 14 September 1940, Souvenir edition. In: Oscar Osburn Winther, *The Transportation Frontier*, 65.
28. Ralph Moody, *Stagecoach West*, 28.
29. Capt. William Banning and George Hugh Banning, *Six Horses*, 368.
30. Ibid., 401-402.

31. Ibid., 361, 363-364. Two excellent sources on the art of driving are William and George Banning, *Six Horses*, and Ralph Moody, *Stagecoach West*.
32. Press-Argus, Centennial Edition, Section C, 12.
33. J.G. Player-Frowd, "Six Months in California," 11. In: Winther, *The Transportation Frontier*, 66.
34. Ormsby, 124.
35. Ibid., 124-125.
36. Nevin, *The Expressmen*, 170.
37. Ibid.
38. Ibid., 129.
39. Root and Connelley, *The Overland Stage to California*, 72.
40. Oliver W. Holmes, Ed., "James A. Garfield's Diary of a Trip to Montana in 1872," Winter 1934-1935, 163. In Winther, *The Transportation Frontier*, 65.
41. Clayton W. Williams, *Texas' Last Frontier. Fort Stockton & the Trans-Pecos, 1861-1895*, 280.
42. Roscoe P. Conkling and Margaret B. Conkling, *The Butterfield Overland Mail, 1857-1869*, I: 375; and Ormsby, 68.
43. John C. Duval, *The Adventures of Big-Foot Wallace*, xiii-xix.
44. Henry W. Daly, "A Dangerous Dash Down Lancaster Hill," *Frontier Times*, 167.
45. Root and Connelley, 464-465. (Used here by permission of Robert McCoy.)
46. James B. Gillett, *Six Years With the Texas Rangers. 1875 to 1881*, 148.

CHAPTER TEN
"He beats the world on staging now . . . ."

"You ask me for our leader;
I'll soon inform you, then;
It's Holladay they call him,
and often only Ben . . . ."

"We have just received notice that the Butterfield route is cut up by the roots . . . It is stopped in all its stages through the state of Texas."[2]

Long before that startling message was read on the floor of Congress in early March of 1861, John Butterfield was in trouble.

It might be recalled that the southern route through Texas was not the path he had bid on. But, he took his contract and, despite the skeptics and seers of doom, made the best of it. With only a year to put the world's "longest stage ride" into operation, the impossible was achieved and the service went on line, on time.

In the forty-four months since, the Southern Overland Mail carried tens of thousands of letters and hundreds of passengers without loss of life and few instances of lost mail. The efficiency of the line improved with each trip until, by February of 1859, the eastbound mails were arriving regularly in St. Louis in twenty-three days, then twenty-two. By late

April of that year, the Missouri *Republican* was reporting an "Extraordinary Dispatch!" with the mail arriving in only twenty-one days and eight hours from San Francisco.[3] The time, almost four full days under the contract time, was duplicated on the next trip and quick runs on the overland became commonplace.

The detractors, however, never stilled their attacks against the "Ox-Bow." Californians, even as they received their mail and newspapers from the East with increasingly more recent dates, continued their demand for even faster service. They argued that what was currently being received in twenty-two or twenty-three days could be received in only sixteen if the route was shortened by cutting out the swing through Texas.

"It was a stupid blunder if nothing worse, on the part of the Administration," went a scathing editorial in the San Francisco *Bulletin*, "which compelled the contractors to take the circuitous route from St. Louis via Memphis and El Paso to San Francisco. Butterfield . . . would have much preferred to take the most direct, available route between the great centers of population . . . But sectional purposes prevailed over right and reason. The Administration was desirous of carrying the route in such direction as should benefit Southern interests, in the idea that the future Pacific Railroad would be sure to follow the track of the mail coaches."[4]

Despite the success and efficiency of the line, the operation was terribly expensive. Butterfield once calculated that it cost more than $60.00 to send a single letter over the road. Just keeping the raided stations stocked with relays and forage was an outlay that had not been reckoned with. When the postmaster general's report for 1860 came out that December, it showed only $170,825 in receipts against the $600,000 for the yearly contract allocation.[5]

Butterfield's one-time partners, Henry Wells and William Fargo, had extended him several loans, but the point was finally reached when the stage pioneer could no longer repay them. Butterfield was removed as president of the company in 1860 and plans were made to shift the operation to the Central route.

John Butterfield's health and spirit gradually went down. In 1867 he suffered a stroke and lingered for two years before succumbing just four days short of his 68th birthday.

Meanwhile, a new post office appropriation bill had become law on March 2, 1861, which called for the discontinuance of the Southern route and its removal to the Central, where it went into effect that summer. It was all academic anyway. Just the week before, Texans had voted to secede from the Union as the nation plunged toward civil war, and the line was shut down anyway.

On March 9 the last eastbound coach pulled away from the big Butterfield station in El Paso. One of the passengers on board was Anson Mills. Born in Indiana, Mills had been an integral part of El Paso's roots, having surveyed the townsite and suggesting the name by which it is still known. He had also built the grand stage station. But, strongly pro-Union, his had been one of only two votes cast against secession in town and he had no choice but to catch this last coach.

Seven other passengers shared the coach, their alliances a tossup between North and South. But, all had agreed to stick together should they run into any trouble along the way. Near Fort Chadbourne, the coach was stopped by a force of Texans under the command of Henry McCullough. For a few tense moments, everyone on board was apprehensive as "it was rumored they would seize the mail company horses for cavalry," wrote Mills. But, after checking the passengers and satisfying themselves that Horace Greeley was not on board (that editor having made some inflammatory remarks about Texas), the militia allowed the coach to continue and Butterfield's Southern Overland Mail line in Texas became history.[6]

The Ox-Bow route was torn asunder. Up and down the line, stations were evacuated and employees scattered according to their allegiances. Those loyal to the Union rounded up the stock and vehicles and began heading to the nearest sympathetic area. Sometimes, the Texans reached the stations first and confiscated animals and equipment.

By as early as mid-April, when Noah Smithwick and other Unionists started on the trail to California, the Butterfield stands along the road were deserted and already in a sad state of ruin. Coaches were still running, however, between San Antonio and El Paso despite the absence of military protection. Smithwick recalled "how eagerly the stage was watched for, and how breathlessly we listened for the latest news of the war that was then only just beginning to take shape."[7]

Due to Union occupation in New Mexico Territory, El Paso was the end of the line. Californians would not receive any mail by way of land until July, when the first daily mail of the Central Overland Company left St. Joseph, Missouri, on July 1 and arrived in San Francisco on the 18th. One through passenger hailed it as "the avant-courier of the great railroad line."[8] But now, southern California wasn't happy, cut off as they were from a direct overland service and one Los Angeles newspaper called the new route a "gigantic humbug and swindle."[9]

By 1862 the Central Overland found itself in the same financial straits as its predecessor and, on March 21, the contract for the portion between Atchison and Salt Lake City was transferred to one Ben Holladay, who changed the name to the Overland Stage Line. Thus entered one of the most colorful and controversial characters in the history of American stage-coaching.

He was born in 1819 in Kentucky, one of seven children to a poor farmer, and decided early on that living from season to season was not for him. At sixteen, he left home and headed west for his fortunes. They began with a menial job in a general store in Weston, Missouri, just across the Missouri River from Fort Leavenworth, Kansas. Before he was out of his teens he was running his own saloon. By the time he was twenty-one, he owned a drugstore and a hotel.

Never one to ignore a gamble, he mortgaged all his property in 1846 and purchased fourteen wagons and sixty mules and, with a load of cargo, headed for Santa Fe in the fledgling United States Territory of New Mexico, where his profits on the cargo staked him to bigger things. Three years later he hauled goods to the recently established Morman town of Salt

Lake City and not only realized the same success as before, but gained the trust of the Saints, not an easy accomplishment for nonbelievers in those days. Next came an extremely profitable venture in cattle in California, taking advantage of the boom that had hit there following the big gold find. Ben Holladay was off and running.

In 1859 he joined forces with William Russell, senior partner in the giant freighting outfit of Russell, Majors & Waddell. Russell didn't like Holladay, and vice versa, but the merger of the two shrewd business minds made killings in the freighting and trading world.

By 1861 Holladay was Russell's biggest creditor and owing to his dislike of the man (Russell had turned him down for a loan when the latter was getting started in the freighting business) and his penchant for distancing friendship from business, Holladay was ready to take full advantage of the situation. The following March he purchased the Central Overland's assets for just $100,000, that portion that stretched some 1,200 miles from Atchison to Salt Lake City, accounting for a little more than half the overland route to California. He also changed the route slightly further south from its previous track along the North Platte River.

Holladay hired the best drivers in the business and paid them princely wages for their loyalty, $100 a month during normal times, twice that when Indians were giving trouble, which was most of the time. He dressed them according to their stature: velvet-trimmed corduroy uniforms, high-heeled boots and wide-brimmed sombreros. In the winter, every man was equipped with an Irish wool overcoat lined with blue flannel. In time, the drivers became fiercely devoted to their boss and often treated passengers to verses of the "Song of the Overland Stage-Driver" (see Chapter Nine). Naturally, Holladay's favorite verse was that one rendered most often:

> *"You ask me for our leader; I'll soon inform you, then;*
> *It's Holladay they call him, and often only Ben;*
> *If you can read the papers, it's easy work to scan*
> *He beats the world on staging now, 'or any other man'."*[10]

Time and schedules were of the utmost importance to Holladay, the animals be hanged. The drivers were expected to maintain an average speed of five miles per hour. A steady trot on the roads was fine, but Holladay wanted whipping, running starts and finishes. The mail contract called for the 1,200 miles between Atchison and Salt Lake City to be run in eleven days. (It was thence six more days from Salt Lake to Placerville, California, on the Central Overland.)

In an attempt to get a bigger government subsidy, Holladay set out to prove that the eleven days could be bettered. He took his own coach from Salt Lake to Atchison in just eight days, six hours. On another occasion, he raced his coach from San Francisco to Atchison in just twelve days, leaving behind a trail—$20,000 worth—of dead and ruined horses.

Mark Twain recounted a story about Holladay's legendary speed. During one of his travels in the West, three years after Holladay began putting his brand on overland staging, Twain shared a coach with a nineteen-year-old boy named Jack and a church elder. Jack had not been raised in the scriptures, knew nothing of them. The elder was just the reverse and his enthusiasm for The Word increased with every mile across the deserts, which he likened to the Holy Land itself. With unbridled enthusiasm, he explained how Moses led the Hebrews 300 miles across the wilderness for forty years before reaching the promised land. "Think of it, Jack!," the good man beamed.

But Jack was not the least bit impressed. "Forty years?" he scoffed. "Only three hundred miles? Humph! Ben Holliday [sic] would have fetched them through in thirty-six hours!"[11]

Holladay proved that he was not above hiring ruthless men to run his efficient machine. Later in 1862 he acquired an additional 200 miles of staging between Julesburg, Colorado, and Wyoming, but discovered that the stretch was plagued by crooked employees and bandits. To run the division, Holladay hired Joseph "Captain Jack" Slade. A fugitive for murder in Illinois, Slade was said to have killed as many as twenty-six men. Given full rein to do whatever was needed, Slade added a few more notches to his gun. Soon, that division was running like a well-oiled machine. But as Mark Twain, in his own inimitable wit, explained: "True, in order to bring about this wholesome change, Slade had to kill several men . . . . but the world was the richer for their loss."[12]

Holladay promptly gave Slade another 400 miles to run, but the hard-drinking outlaw ran afoul of the United States Army and Holladay was forced to fire him. Eventually, Slade ran afoul of the residents of Virginia City, Montana, as well and was hanged for disorderly conduct.[13]

By now Holladay's reputation fit perfectly his own physical stature. Tall and large-framed, he had a booming voice to match. One contemporary described him as "good looking and picturesque," but another said he was "illiterate, coarse, boastful, false and cunning!"[14]

Holladay overpowered opponents by intimidation and cunning and anyone with aspirations on starting a staging line anywhere in his vicinity was soon discouraged and it didn't seem to matter who they were. Not even a Denver sheriff.

To supplement his income, this lawman ran a feeder line between the capital and the mining town of Central City, a distance of about 30 miles. He charged only $6.00 and had a good business. Holladay decided he wanted it and quickly put his own coaches on the road and charged $2.00. Of course, the sheriff could not afford to run his line at such rates and folded. With him out of the way, Holladay upped his fares to $12.00, took off the comfortable Concords, and substituted double-decker omnibuses. No matter that they took twice as long to make the trip; Holladay's was the only game in town.

He continued to swallow up stagecoach lines whenever and wherever he chose. Gold strikes in Montana and Idaho in 1862 and 1863 created the need for a service north of Salt Lake City. Three operations went into business, each charging $150 per passenger on the 400-mile run. There was enough business for all three, but Holladay decided he wanted it. Alone. A quick trip to Washington D.C. to visit with postmaster general Montgomery Blair produced a contract to carry the mail between Salt Lake and Walla Walla in Washington Territory via the goldfields, plus another contract for service to Virginia City, Montana. Holladay was in business.

He set his fares between Salt Lake City and Virginia City at $25.00. He could afford to run at a loss for a while; the others could not. Within three months, two of them folded; the third, a man named Oliver, not only had the gall to resist, but brazenly opened up a new stretch of line 120 miles from Virginia City to Helena, operated new coaches, and charged $25.00.

Furious, Holladay put new Concords on the new road and charged $2.50! It took only two months for poor Oliver to holler "uncle." Now solidly in charge of staging in the Big Sky Country, Holladay followed with his usual pattern. He replaced his grand Concords with 20-passenger wagons, raised the fare to $37.50, and even reduced the frequency of departures. The traveling public cursed and wailed loudly, but to no avail.

In the same manner that Holladay liquidated competition, he could make or break a town. When the little Kansas stage stop town of Marysville refused to build a road and bridge on the outskirts of town over Spring Creek and suggested that Holladay build his own, he promptly cut the village from his schedule and bypassed it altogether. The residents burned Holladay in effigy, cut loose a ferry he had built on the Big Blue River, and dug a trench across the stage road. The latter act only resulted in the deaths of some innocent horses when a night coach fell in. And it did nothing to sway Holladay; he simply requested an army escort. Finally, the town surrendered and built the road and the bridge. Holladay, never one to forgive easily, waited five months to return Marysville to his schedule.

Meanwhile, other stage lines fell to his brand of intimidation, including the Western Stage Company that operated a line between Omaha and Fort Kearney. It wasn't a big line, but Holladay coveted it. When Western wouldn't sell to him, Holladay refused to take their passengers connecting at Fort Kearney with his coaches. Western's owners appealed to the postmaster general who then ordered Holladay to accept those passengers any and every time he had room. Holladay agreed. And then saw to it that he never had the room, filling up any empty seats with company employees. Finally, Western sold out to Holladay and, as usual, at his price.

Fittingly enclosed by a laurel wreath, Ben Holladay dominates this 1864 advertisement for his Overland Stage Line. Notice that Holladay coaches connected at Denver for tri-weekly service to New Mexico, although it is not clear whether he owned that route as well. The coach shown in the photo at bottom is a Celerity. (Courtesy of The Bancroft Library, University of California at Berkeley)

Denver's *Rocky Mountain News* called him a "nuisance." A competitor, most likely a short-lived one, said he was "wholly destitute of honesty, morality and common decency." But *Harper's Weekly,* no doubt far removed from the situation, said that he was "the greatest organizer of transportation the west has produced."[15]

In Holladay, the Bannings saw both the best and the worst. "He was not a Birch or a Butterfield," they wrote, "but still he was a shrewd businessman, with faults of disposition and education, often haughty and dictatorial. A man inspired by a love of amassing a fortune, he would tackle anything which would gain him that end."[16]

By now, Ben Holladay may not have been the most liked man in the West, but he was about the richest and most powerful. Altogether he operated more than 3,000 miles of stagecoach and freight lines in Kansas, Nebraska, Colorado, Nevada, Utah, Oregon, Idaho, the Northwest, and Montana; had 15,000 employees, 20,000 vehicles (including 110 Concords), and 150,000 animals. Despite the fact that he suffered huge financial losses to Indian depredations, he still grossed enough from his passenger and express receipts (the latter which he carried under contracts with the country's three leading express agencies: Wells, Fargo; American Express; and United States Express) that he survived what sent other carriers to ruin.

He also owned 16 Pacific steamers; slaughter houses, packing plants, grain mills, general stores, and even gold and silver mines; and three lavish homes, one each in Washington D.C., New York City, and a 200-room palace near White Plains, New York.[17]

Then, late in 1865, one David Butterfield, no relation to John, came upon the scene. The former Denver merchant had two big things going for him: a goodly amount of capital and contracts with Holladay's three big express customers who had become disenchanted with his dealings. With a start of $3 million, Butterfield opened a line between Atchison, Fort Leavenworth, and Denver, to run along the Smokey Hill River, some 100 miles south of the Platte. The new route actually cut

61 miles off of Holladay's more northerly route, and therefore saved time.

Almost immediately, the new line, called the Butterfield Overland Despatch, began having Indian problems. Stagecoaches were attacked, passengers and strongboxes robbed. But it didn't escape the notice of anyone that the raiders acted very "unIndianish." Right away, charges flew that the Indians were actually some of Holladay's hirelings dressed as braves. When real Indians starting raiding his line and two employees were killed at a stage station, passengers began to stay away from the Overland Despatch.

Between Holladay and the Indians, Butterfield was in trouble by January of 1866. That month, the company was reorganized and Butterfield was retained as general manager. Wells, Fargo was behind the reorganization, backed by the other two express giants. They made it clear that they would set up their own stage line between Salt Lake City and Denver to connect with the Despatch if Holladay didn't start carrying their express shipments on *their* terms.

Holladay went into a rage. In New York City, he invited banker David Bray to lunch. Bray, who was also president of the Overland Despatch, never got to enjoy his meal. Holladay soon had him so bullied that the stage line was his by nightfall, whereupon he telegraphed Wells, Fargo and associates and told them to go right ahead and start their service between Denver and Salt Lake City and "be damned!"[18]

In March the merger was complete and the name changed to the Holladay Overland Mail and Express Company.

Curiously, Holladay gained control of the Despatch when he knew that the end of overland staging was near. The consensus in most quarters was that linking the country with the railroad was another decade off. But Holladay knew better even though only forty miles of Union Pacific rails had been laid west of Omaha by May of 1866. But the action picked up quickly over the summer. Now, rails were being laid four to the minute, 400 to the mile. By fall, the Union Pacific had reached the 100th meridian, 247 miles from Omaha. Although it would be three years before the U.P. linked with the Central

Pacific pushing eastward across the Sierras, some seven years sooner than many were predicting, Holladay decided not to wait.

He raised the express rates on gold shipments and likewise hiked passenger fares on the Atchison to Salt Lake City run from $150 to $350, all apparently an endeavor to squeeze the last ounce of blood out of the turnip. Then, on November 1, only eight months after taking over the Despatch, Holladay sold his empire to Wells, Fargo for $1.5 million in cash plus $300,000 in Wells, Fargo stock and a seat on the Board of Directors. What he had always purchased for songs he now sold for a symphony.

It would seem that Holladay had the last laugh. Wells, Fargo was among those who predicted the linking of the rails still a decade away. As late as 1867 they still saw no immediate threat to stagecoaching from the two railroads that inched ever closer together. In April of 1868 Wells, Fargo even ordered thirty brand new Concords which were delivered to the western railhead, by now in Wyoming.

Only a month after receiving shipment of the new stage-coaches, Wells, Fargo suddenly sold its entire stage operation, coaches, animals, tack, everything. Only a year later, on May 10, 1869, the Union and Central Pacific railroads joined in northern Utah. Overland stagecoaching was no more.

Wells, Fargo, founded in San Francisco in 1852, and well known for its honesty and reliability, continued to operate thousands of miles of stage lines in California and other points in the West for years. They survived because they changed as the West changed. But what of Ben Holladay?

After selling his stagecoach empire, Holladay moved to Oregon. Not one to rest upon his laurels, or his riches, he went into steamboating, eventually owning nine paddlewheelers on Oregon rivers. He even indulged in railroading with the Oregon and California Railroad. He built another palatial home in Portland from which he attempted to realize his newest ambition—to be U.S. Senator. Though the voters wisely turned him down, he managed to handpick who went to Washington.

PHOTOGRAPHIC VIEW OF

Coaches shipped by Abbot, Downing & Co., Concord, N. H.

This photo is one of ironies. In April of 1868 a trainload of 30 brand new Concord stagecoaches was carried to a rail-head on the Missouri River for delivery to Wells, Fargo & Company. A year later, the rails that linked a continent were completed and overland stagecoaching become obsolete. Wells, Fargo itself, shortly after receiving this shipment of coaches, sold all its stage lines. (Courtesy New Hampshire Historical Society)

But even Holladay was not immune to disaster. On September 18, 1873 the New York stock market crashed and with it, Holladay's empire. On the same day he defaulted on the Oregon and California Railroad bonds, his beloved wife Ann died. Further, none of their four children lived to middle age. One daughter died in childbirth, another died after taking ill on board a ship bound for New York, and both sons died alcoholics.

A year after Ann's death, Holladay remarried and they had two children. With renewed vigor, he tried a comeback, but was hampered by a brother who claimed title to what little of the properties was left. Frustrated and humbled, just as he had left his opponents, Ben Holladay died in 1887 at the age of 68.

A letter published in the St. Joseph *Catholic Tribune* on June 22, 1895 praised him for his accomplishments and the writer could have been talking about any of the stage men who took their risks in the West.

"His [Holladay's] life showed the elasticity of American institutions: At fifteen, laboring on a farm in . . . Kentucky; at forty, owned sixteen steamships, trading to every point of the Pacific."[19]

Genius or illiterate? Shrewd or immoral? Whatever the final judgement history passes on to Ben Holladay, he was the last of a remarkable breed of men who filled a vast space in the westward movement of this country.

Notes, Chapter Ten

1. Frank A. Root and William Elsey Connelley, *The Overland Stage to California*, 465.
2. U.S. *Congressional Globe*, 36th Congress, Second Session, 1112. In: LeRoy R. Hafen, *The Overland Mail*, 1849-1869, 213.
3. Missouri *Republican*, 26 April 1859.
4. San Francisco *Bulletin*, 31 January 1860.
5. Postmaster General's Report, 1860, 436. U.S. Senate, Executive Documents, 36th Congress, Second Session, No. 1, Part iii, Serial No. 1080.
6. Anson Mills, *My Story*, 64. Mills would return to El Paso after the war and continue to be a major factor in the city's development.
7. Noah Smithwick, *The Evolution of a State*, 335, 339.
8. Root and Connelley, 43.
9. Roscoe P. Conkling and Margaret B. Conkling, *The Butterfield Overland Mail, 1857-1869*, II:341.
10. Root and Connelley, 465.
11. Mark Twain, *Roughing It*, 27-28.
12. Ibid., 71
13. David Nevin, *The Expressmen*, 139.
14. George A. Thompson, *Throw Down the Box!*, 21.
15. Nevin, 123.
16. Captain William Banning and George Hugh Banning, *Six Horses*. In Thompson, 21.
17. Nevin, 127.
18. Ibid., 143-144.
19. St. Joseph *Catholic Tribune*, 22 June 1895. In Root and Connelley, 451.

EPILOGUE
" . . . good bye John . . . . "

"The coach stands rusting in the yard,
And the horse has sought the plow;
We have spanned the world with an iron rail,
And the Steam King rules us now."[1]

As far as the Southern Overland was concerned, the Civil War only ended what would have eventually been accomplished by the railroads anyway. Some East Texas stage lines had been displaced even before the war. An early line, between Marshall and Shreveport, Louisiana, was eliminated as early as February of 1858 with the completion of the Southern Pacific Railroad. That same month, Texas had 117 miles of railroad finished and 75 more miles graded, ". . . one fifth of all there is west of the Mississippi river . . . ."[2]

San Antonioans eagerly anticipated the rails that were rapidly nearing the city from the Gulf Coast. On that subject, a correspondent of the *Herald* wrote from Halletsville that while the little town's citizens were delighted with the news from California that came by the quick San Diego coaches, they were looking forward to being able to travel to San Antonio in only four or five hours by train.

"We are just on the eve of a mighty railroad spirit in Texas," he wrote, "and San Antonio is to be benefitted more than any other point thereby, from the fact that she will be without a competitor for the great and growing Western trade."[3]

Slowly, but surely, the advance of the rails preempted the stagecoach routes, often over the ruts of the old coach roads themselves.

Rail laying, which had come to a virtual stop in Texas during the war, accelerated afterwards. By late March 1868, there were a little over 500 miles of railroads in the state in running order. Two years later San Antonioans were excited about the building of the Southern Transcontinental Railroad from Galveston all the way to San Diego, California. George Giddings, the old stage man who knew when to change with the times, was said to be the power behind the project and predicted that this "great national highway would be the making of San Antonio and western Texas."[4]

In the late 1870s some Texas points were still connected with Yuma, Arizona, by long-distance staging. Said then to be the longest *daily* stage line in the world, at 1,560 miles, was the Fort Worth and Yuma Stage Line, contracted in 1877, with J. T. Chidester as agent. Originally set to run in 17 days, it was soon determined that this took too long. "The coyotes, jackrabbits and horned frogs that were the principal inhabitants of the country beyond the Conchos could not afford to wait that long for their mail . . .," Chidester wrote facetiously.[5]

The Postal Department agreed to double the contractor's compensation if he could run the route in thirteen days, and this was done even though trouble with Indians remained. The stage line was discontinued when the Texas and Pacific Railway laid tracks west of Fort Worth. The T&P was completed as far as Big Spring in 1881 and served as a feeder to the local stage lines connecting with it.

By the end of December 1881, San Antonio newspapers no longer carried advertisements for the overland stagecoach lines. On January 1, 1882, the Texas & Pacific reached El Paso and the grand old stage route of more than three decades was no more.

When the rails from Los Angeles and Fort Worth met at Sierra Blanca, about 100 miles east of El Paso, in the early 1880s, any reason for long-distance stage operations in Texas ceased to exist. Isolated towns continued to get coach service, usually connecting with a railroad.[6]

Stagecoaches were still operating in some parts of the state even after the turn of the century. One long running line supplied mail and passengers between Comstock, near the Rio Grande, and Ozona, in present Crockett County, as late as 1905. The railroad passed through Comstock where a coach connection was made for the eighty-mile stage to Ozona. Among the stations along the way was a ranch house owned by James Sheppard Baker and where Mrs. Baker had contracted to feed stage passengers. Progress does have its rewards; instead of a horn announcing a stage's approach, the agent at Comstock would telephone Mrs. Baker and let her know if there were any passengers on board, how many, and give their estimated time of arrival.[7]

A line between Brownsville and Alice continued to operate up to 1904, when the Gulf Coast Lines Railway arrived at the extreme southern Texas town. Knickerbocker, in Tom Green County, twenty miles southwest of San Angelo, continued to get its mail by coach as late as 1920.

Stagecoaches were still running in West Texas to the late 1800s. (Courtesy Fort Concho National Historic Landmark)

The same was true throughout the West. The old "cradle on wheels" hung on to its existence tenaciously. Wells, Fargo coaches were still carrying passengers and mail to and from the Nevada gold claims in 1904 and continued to work for a few years after the railroad reached Goldfield, Nevada, that same year.

Most people were happy to see the rails replace the ruts. A passenger who stepped off a train in New Orleans in October of 1859 was amazed that he was only eighty-six hours from New York City, including forty-eight miles of stage travel which alone took half a day. He went on to say that when that portion was filled in by rail, it would save another ten hours. "And when that is completed," he gloated, "and a Rail-road connection [made] from [San Antonio] to New Orleans, then good bye John, to lumbering stagecoaches . . . ."[8]

Reflecting upon his many travels in the West, Albert Richardson was glad to say "good bye John" to the stagecoach and welcome to the railroad. "Having traveled to Fort Kearney seven times by wagon and coach," he wrote, "I found accomplishing it by rail in a few hours decidedly agreeable."[9]

Another frequent traveler, a correspondent for the San Antonio *Daily Herald* named George H. Sweet, wrote scathingly of, what seemed to him, a snail's pace in replacing the stagecoach with the railroad. In 1868 he took the Central Railroad from Houston and arrived at Cypress City, 25 miles away, in a little over an hour. At Cypress City he boarded a stagecoach and arrived at Montgomery, 30 miles distant, after a ride of 10½ hours. "Comment is unnecessary," he wrote. "—it is the old story of the stage ride, and one stage ride is as good as another. The railroad is civilization—the stage is barbarism . . . When will Texans in every part of the State arouse themselves to the successful effort of abolishing the latter and inaugurating the former? . . . there will be no royal prosperity for Texas or Texans, until railroads abolish our magnificent distances, cheapen our rates of transportation, [and] carry our mails quicker and more reliably . . . ."[22]

Not everyone, however, was thrilled about the ending of the old way. H. H. McConnell was melancholy about its passing. "No modern invention of vestibule cars or other improved appliances of travel," he wrote, "can equal for sociability and pleasure the old stagecoach when time was of no particular importance, and where the passengers were congenial and thrown together long enough to strike up a sort of an acquaintance . . . ."[11]

A guide to Southern and Western Texas written in 1878 romanticized that dying mode of travel. The author had journeyed from San Antonio to Fredericksburg on a four-horse coach of the Charles Bain & Company stage line (this outfit was the main firm in Texas during the twilight years of staging), and looked upon the ride between old Bexar and the little Hill Country town as the best portion of the trip that had included riding the rails.

"After one has been whirled through dust, cinders and smoke, at the rate of twenty-five miles an hour, for a thousand miles or more, it is a relief to change the rail-car for that dear old relic of the past—the stagecoach—with its four prancing horses, its ever-merry driver with tin horn ever ready to signal a station or a start. From the stagecoach one can see the country, enjoy the scenery along the route, and be sociable without splitting one's throat in the endeavor to be heard above the din and rattle, as is the case in railroad traveling . . . there is a luxury in that medium of traveling that neither time nor improvements can efface."[12]

An unknown writer for the Atchison *Champion* spoke eloquently of its passing:

"There are few if any of the things of the fading past to which in our reminiscent moods, we revert more fondly than the old stagecoach . . .," he began.

"The old stagecoach! How well we remember it, and how vividly we recall its appearance . . . It seemed to us then the very incarnation of cosiness [sic] and comfort, the embodiment of all that was best in the line of transportation . . . But the old stagecoach has ended its career—made its last trip . . . .

"Poor old coach! there it stands, one of the most magnificent 'has beens' of a romantic period of our lives."[13]

Neglect its reward for years of service, the 'General Sam Houston' stage rots in a yard. This coach was well known in Texas and operated out of Austin for many years. The coach belonged to Monroe Miller, who owned the Eclipse Stables, located on East 7th in the capital city. The company was founded in 1855 by John T. Miller; his son, Monroe, took over the business in 1872. The 'General Sam Houston' coach made its first run between Austin and Brenham in 1841. The Concord was in use for many years; it is known to have made trips to Round Rock in 1876. The coach was finally 'retired' and in the state shown here around the turn of the century. (Courtesy Texas State Archives)

The End

Notes, Epilogue

1. Richard F. Palmer, *The 'Old Line Mail'. Stagecoach Days in Upstate New York*, 136. Poem is used through the courtesy of North Country Books.
2. San Antonio *Herald*, 6 February 1858.
3. Ibid., 20 July 1858.
4. San Antonio *Daily Herald*, 3 January 1868.
5. Capt. B. B. Paddock, Ed., *History of Texas, Fort Worth and the Texas Northwest Edition*, 624-625.
6. J. W. Williams, *Old Texas Trails*, 387. Williams is an excellent source for a detailed account of the spiderweb of stage lines in North and West Texas during the coming of the railroads and their eventual demise.
7. Kathryn Turner Carter, *Stagecoach Inns of Texas*, 88.
8. San Antonio *Herald*, 8 October 1859.
9. Albert D. Richardson, *Beyond the Mississippi: From the Great River to the Great Ocean*, 566.
10. San Antonio *Daily Herald*, 4 June 1868.
11. H. H. McConnell, *Five Years a Cavalryman*, 271.
12. James L. Rock and W. I. Smith, *Southern and Western Texas Guide for 1878*, 240.
13. Frank A. Root and William Elsey Connelley, *The Overland Stage to California*, 598-599.

APPENDIX A
Routes

Approximate mileages shown between stations; accumulative distances in ( ). In many cases, stations were later added or deleted.

Table 1. The Butterfield (Southern) Overland Mail

The following breakdown of the Butterfield Overland Route (original route) stations into divisions was made by G. Bailey, a special agent to Postmaster General Aaron V. Brown who accompanied the first eastbound mail. (Source: Roscoe P. and Margaret B. Conkling, *The Butterfield Overland Mail, 1857-1869*)

FIRST DIVISION

San Francisco (CA) to Clark's, 12 miles; San Mateo, 9; Redwood City, 9; Mountain View, 12; San Jose, 11; Seventeen Mile House, 17; Gilroy, 13; Pacheco Pass, 18; St.Louis Ranch, 17; Lone Willow, 18; Temple's Ranch, 13; Firebaugh's Ferry, 12; Fresno City, 19; Elk Horn Spring, 22; Whitmore's Ferry, 17; Cross Creek, 12; Visalia, 12 (243); Packwood, 12; Tule River, 14; Fountain Spring, 14; Mountain House, 12; Posey Creek, 15; Gordon's Ferry, 10; Kern River Slough, 12; Sink of Tejon, 14; Fort Tejon, 16 (362); Reed's, 8; French John's, 14; Widow Smith's, 24; King's, 10; Hart's, 12; San Fernando Mission, 8; Cahuengo, 12; Los Angeles, 12 (462). Total, 462 miles. Time, 80 hours.

SECOND DIVISION

Los Angeles to Monte, 13 miles; San Jose, 12; Chino Ranch, 12; Temascal, 20; Laguna Grande, 10; Temecula, 21; Tejungo, 14; Oak Grove, 12; Warner's Ranch, 10; San Felipe, 16; Vallecito, 18; Palm Springs, 9; Carrizo Creek, 9; Indian Wells, 32; Alamo Mocho, 24; Cook's Wells, 22; Pilot Knob, 18; Fort Yuma (AZ), 10 (744). Total, 282 miles. Time, 72 hrs., 20 minutes.

(Note: There is no water on this route between Carrizo creek and the Colorado, except at the stations.)

THIRD DIVISION

Fort Yuma to Swiveller's Ranch, 20 miles; Fillibuster Camp, 18; Peterman's 19; Griswell's 12; Flap-Jack Ranch, 15; Oatman Flat, 20; Murderer's Grave, 20; Gila Ranch, 17; Maricopa Wells, 40; Sacatoon, 22; Picacho del Tucson, 37; Pointer Mountain (Charcos de los Pimas), 22; Tucson, 18 (1024). Total, 280 miles. Time, 71 hrs., 45 min.

FOURTH DIVISION

Tucson to Seneca Springs (Cienega de los Pimas), 35 miles; San Pedro river, 24; Dragoon Springs, 23; Apache Pass (Puerto del Dado), 40; Stein's Peak, (NM) 35; Soldier's Farewell, 42 (1223); Ojo de la Vaca, 14; Mimbres river, 16; Cook's Spring, 18; Picacho (opposite Dona Ana), 52; Fort Fillmore, 14; Cottonwoods, (TX) 25; Franklin (El Paso), 22 (1384). Total, 360 miles. Time, 82 hrs.

(Note: There is no water on this route between Tucson and the Rio Grande, except at the stations.)

FIFTH DIVISION

Franklin to Waco [Hueco] Tanks, 30 miles; Cornudos de los Alamos, 36; Pinery, 56; Delaware Springs, 24; Pope's Camp, 40 (1570); Emigrant Crossing, 65; Horse Head Crossing, 55; Head of Concho, 70; Camp (_____), 30; Grape Creek, 22; Fort Chadbourne, 30 (1842). Total, 458 miles. Time, 126 hrs., 30 min.

(Note: There is no water on the route between Franklin and Pope's Camp, and between Horse Head Crossing and the

Mustang Ponds, near the head of Concho, except at the stations.)

SIXTH DIVISION

Fort Chadbourne to Valley Creek, 12 miles; Mountain Pass, 16; Phantom Hill, 30; Smith's, 12; Clear Fork (of the Brazos), 26; Franz's, 13; Fort Belknap, 22; Murphy's, 16; Jacksboro, 19 (2008); Earhart's, 16; Conolly's, 16; Davidson's 24; Gainesville, 17; Diamond's, 15; Sherman, 15; Colbert's Ferry (Red River), (IT) 13½ (2124½). Total, 282½ miles. Time, 65 hrs., 25 min.

SEVENTH DIVISION

Colbert's Ferry to Fisher's, 13 miles; Nale's, 14; Boggy Depot, 17; Gary's, 16; Waddell's, 15; Blackburn's, 16; Pusley's, 17; Riddell's, 16; Halloway's, 18; Trayon's, 19; Walker's (Choctaw agency), 16; Fort Smith, (ARK) 15 (2316½). Total, 192 miles. Time, 38 hrs.

EIGHTH DIVISION

Fort Smith to Woosley's, 16 miles; Brodie's, 12; Park's, 20; Fayetteville, 14; Fitzgerald's, 12; Callaghan's, 22; Harburn's, (MO) 19; Couch's, 16; Smith's, 15; Ashmore's, 20; Springfield, 13 (2495½); Evan's, 9; Smith's, 11; Bolivar, 11½; Yost's, 16; Quincy, 16; Bailey's, 10; Warsaw, 11; Burn's, 15; Mulholland's, 20; Shackelford's, 13; Tipton, 7 (2635). Total, 318½ miles. Time, 48 hrs., 55 min.

NINTH DIVISION

Tipton to St. Louis (by Pacific railroad), 160 miles. Time, 11 hrs., 40 min.

Recap: Total, 2,795 miles. Time, 595 hrs., 15 min. (Bailey deducted 2 hrs., 9 min., for time difference between the east and west terminals resulting in an actual travel time on the first trip of 24 days, 18 hrs., 26 min.)

Table 2. The San Antonio &
San Diego Mail Route

Lower Road
(Source: Captain William & George H. Banning, *Six Horses*,
and the 1859 *Texas Almanac*.)

San Antonio (TX) to Leon River, 7 miles; Castroville, 18;
D'Hanis (Saco River), 25; Ranchero Creek, 9; Sabinal Creek, 4;
Comanche Creek, 5; Rio Frio, 8; Uvalde, 6 (82); Nueces [River],
9; Turkey Creek, 11; Elm Creek, 15; Fort Clark (Las Moras
Springs), 7 (124); Piedra Pinto, 7; Maveric[k] Creek, 9; San
Felipe [Creek], 12; 1st Crossing San Pedro River, 10; Painted
Caves, 3; Calf Springs, 16; Willow Springs, 2; Fort [Camp]
Hudson, 16 (199); Head of San Pedro River*, 20; Howard
Springs, 44; Live Oak Creek, 30; Fort Lancaster, 3 (296); Pecos
River Crossing, 4; Pecos Springs, 6; Point of leaving Pecos
River, 32; Arroyo Escondido, 16; Escondido Springs, 9; Co-
manche Springs [Fort Stockton], 19 (382); Leone Hole [Leon
Springs], 9; Hackleberry Pond, 11; [Barrilla Station in this
section]; Limpia Creek, 32; Fort Davis, 19 (453); Point of Rocks,
10; Baree [Barrel] Springs, 9; Deadman's Hole, 13; [El Muerto];
Van Horn's Wells, 33; Eagle Springs, 20 (538); [Quitman Can-
yon]; First Camp on Rio Grande, 31; Birchville, 35; San
Elizario, 25; Socorro, 6; Ysleta, 3; El Paso, 14 (652); Cottonwoods, 22 (674).

Cottonwoods to Fort Fillmore (NM), 22 miles, (696); La
Mesilla, 6; Cook's Spring, 65; Rio Mimbres, 18; Ojo de la Vaca,
17; [Soldier's Farewell]; Ojo de Ynez, 10; Peloncillo, 34; Rio
Saur (San Domingo), 18 (864).

Rio Saur to Apache Springs (AZ), 23 miles (887); Dos
Cabesas, 9; Dragoon Springs, 26; Mouth of Quercos Canon, 18;
San Pedro Crossing, 6; Cienega, 20; Cienega Creek, 13; Mission
San Xavier, 20; Tucson, 8 (1007); Charcos de los Pimos, 30;
Picacho [Pass], 5; First Camp on the Gila River, 35; Maricopa
Wells, 29; Tezotal (across El Jornada), 40; Ten-Mile Camp, 10;
Murderer's Grave, 8; Oatman Flat (Gila Crossing), 15; Second

Crossing Gila River, 25; Peterman's Station, 32; Antelope Peak, 20; Little Corral, 24; Fort Yuma, 16 (1296).

Fort Yuma to Pilot Knob (CA), 7 miles (1303); Cook's Wells, 13; Alamo Mocho, 22; Indian Wells, 21; Carrizo Creek, 32; Vallecito, 18; Lassator's Ranch, 17; Julian's [Ranch], 7; William's [Ranch], 7; Ames' [Ranch], 14; Mission San Diego, 16; San Diego, 5 (1475).

*This is not the San Pedro River.

Table 3. Holladay Overland Mail

[Source: George A. Thompson, *Throw Down the Box!*]

Atchison, Kansas to Lancaster, 10 miles; Kennekuk, 14; Kickapoo, 12; Log Chain, 13; Seneca, 11; Laramie Creek, 12; Guittard's, 12; Oketo, 10; Otoe, 11; Pawnee, 11; (116); Grayson's, 14; Big Sandy, 10; Thompson's, 14; Kiowa, 14; Little Blue, 12; Liberty Farm, 13; Lone Tree, 15; 32 Mile Creek, 10; Summit, 12; Hook's, 13; Fort Kearney, 10 (253); Platte Station, 10; Craig, 11; Plum Creek, 15; Willow Island, 15; Midway, 14 (318).

Midway to Gilman's (NEB), 15 miles (333); Cottonwood Springs, 17; Cold Springs, 15; Fremont Springs, 14; Elkhorn, 11; Alkali Lake, 14; Sand Hill, 12; Diamond Springs, 11; South Platte, 15 (442).

South Platte to Julesberg (CO), 14 miles (456); Antelope, 12; Spring Hill, 13l Dennison's, 13; Valley Station, 12; Kelly's, 15; Beaver Creek, 12; Bijou, 20; Fremont's Orchard, 16; Eagle's Nest, 11; Latham, 12; Big Bend, 15; Fort Lupton, 17; Pierson's, 15; Denver, 14 (653); Child's, 11; Boon's, 12; Little Thompson, 18; Big Thompson, 8; Laporte, 16; Boner, 10; Cherokee, 12; Virginia Dale, 12 (752).

Virginia Dale to Willow Springs (WYO), 15 miles (767); Big Laramie, 15; Little Laramie, 14; Cooper Creek, 17; Rock Creek, 11; Medicine Bow, 17; Elk Mountain, 8; Pass Creek, 14; North Platte, 16; Sage Creek, 14; Pine Grove, 10; Bridger's Pass, 9; Sulphur Springs, 10; Washie, 11; Duck Lake, 13; Dug Springs,

12; No Name, 15; Big Pond, 12; Black Buttes, 14; Rock Point, 14 (1013); Salt Wells, 14; Rock Springs, 14; Green River, 15; Lone Tree, 14; Ham's Fork, 18; Church Buttes, 12; Millersville, 8; Fort Bridger, 13 (1121); Muddy, 12; Quaking Aspen Spring, 10; Bear River, 10 (1153).

Bear River to Needle Rocks (UT), 10 miles (1163); Echo Canyon, 10; Hanging Rock, 10; Weber, 10; Daniel's, 12; Kimball's, 11; Mountain Dell, 15; Salt Lake City, 14 (1245); Traveller's Rest, 9; Porter Rockwell's, 11; Joe's Dugout, 9; Camp Floyd, 10; Five Mile, 10; Faust's, 10; Point Lookout, 11; Simpson Springs, 15; Riverbed, 8; Dugway, 10; Black Rock, 12; Fish Springs, 11; Boyd's, 10; Willow Springs (Callao), 10; Canyon, 15; Deep Creek (Ibapah), 12 (1418).

Deep Creek to Prairie Gate (NEV), 8 miles (1426); Antelope Springs, 18; Spring Valley, 13; Schell Creek, 12; Gold Canyon, 12; Butte, 15; Mountain Springs, 11; Ruby Valley, 9; Jacob's Well, 12; Diamond Springs, 12; Sulphur Springs, 12 (1552); Robert's Creek, 13; Camp Station, 13; Dry Creek, 15; Cape Horn, 10; Simpson's Park, 11; Reese River, 15; Mount Airey, 12; Castle Rock, 12; Edward's Creek, 12; Cold Springs, 11; Middle Gate, 16; Fair View, 15; Mountain Well, 13; Still Water, 15; Old River, 14; Bisby's 14; Nevada City, 11; Desert Wells, 12; Dayton, 13; Carson City, 13 (1812); Mormon Station (Genoa), 14; Friday's, 11 (1837).

Friday's to Yank's (CA), 10 miles (1847); Strawberry, 12; Webster's, 12; Moss, 12; Sportsman's Hall, 12; Placerville, 12 (1907); [Thence to Sacramento].

Table 4. Butterfield Overland Despatch (Smokey Hill Route)

[Source: George A. Thompson, *Throw Down the Box!*] Not all station names are known and are left blank.

Fort Riley, Kansas to Junction City, 3 miles; Chapman's Creek, 13; Abilene, 12; Solomon River, 10; ——; Salina, 13; Spring Creek, 15; Ellsworth, 14; Buffalo Creek, 12; ——; Hick's Station 15; ——; Fossil Creek, 15; ——; Forsythes, 11; Big Creek, 11; ——; Louisa, 12; ——; Bluffton, 14; ——; Downer, 13; Castle Rock, 9; Grinnel Springs, 11; Chalk, 12; ——; Monument, 13; Smokey Hill Spring, 11; ——; Eaton, 12; Henshaw, 13; Pond Creek, 11; ——; Willow, 14; ——; Blue Mound, 9; Cheyenne Wells, 13; ——; Dubois, 24; ——; Grady's, 11; ——; Connell, 13; ——; Coon, 12; ——; Hogan Lake, 11; Hedinger (Cedar Point), 9; ——; Big Bend, 13; ——; Reed's Springs, 13; Bijou Creek, 12; Kiowa, 9; Ruthton, 9; ——; Cherry Creek, 16; ——; Denver, 14 (592 miles).

APPENDIX B
Price List of a New Concord Mail Coach, 1870

Mail coach, with leather boots, deck seat, brake, lamps and ornamental sides:

To seat 12 inside	$1,050.00
To seat 9 inside (heavy)	975.00
To seat 9 inside (medium)	900.00
To seat 6 inside (2 or 3 seats)	775.00

Add

For deck seat on rear of coach	20.00
For packing body only	12.00
For packing coach complete	20.00

Deduct

If no brake	25.00
If no lamps	8.00
If no deck seat	20.00
If no ornamental paint	20.00

Hotel coach, with window quarters and baggage binder, leather lining, no brake or lamps:

To seat 12 inside	1,050.00
To seat 9 inside	950.00

Add

For brake	25.00
For plush lining	25.00
For lamps	15.00 to 45.00

[Source: Conkling, *The Butterfield Overland Mail, 1857-1869*]

BIBLIOGRAPHY

DOCUMENTS

Letters Sent, Fort Davis. Lt. Col. Wesley Merritt to Capt. C. E. Morse, December 22, 1868. U.S. Army Commands, R.G. 98, N.A. Roll No. (7675) 6. Fort Davis National Historic Site (FDNHS).

— Lt. Col. William R. Shafter to Maj. A.P. Morrow, February 7, 1872. U.S. Army Commands, RG 98, NA Roll No. 1777. (FDNHS)

— Col. George L. Andrews to Capt. Charles Bentzoni, October 6, 1872. U.S. Army Commands, RG 98, NA Roll No. 1777. (FDNHS)

— 1st. Lt. W.H.W. James to Non-Commissioned Officer, Barilla Springs, August 7, 1880. RG 98, NA Roll (10427) 1. (FDNHS)

— Shafter to Agent F.C. Taylor, ca. 1872. NA Roll No. 1777. (FDNHS)

— James to Non-Commissioned Officer, Barilla Springs, 7 August 1880. NA Roll No. (10427) 1. (FDNHS)

— Regular Army Mobile Units 1821-1942. 8th U.S. Infantry, Col. Washington Seawell, Fort Davis, Texas.

Letters Sent, Fort Concho. Maj. George C. Cram to Col. Edward Hatch, 9 May 1868. RG 98, NARS.

— Cram to Hatch, 25 May 1868. RG 98, NARS.

MAGAZINE ARTICLES

Andrews, Alexander. "Coaching." *Gentleman's Magazine*, VI, n.s., May 1871, 677.

Baylor, George W. "Tragedies on the Old Overland Stage Route." *Frontier Times*, Vol. 26, No. 6, March 1949, 125-128.

Bender, A. B. "Opening Routes Across West Texas, 1848-1850." *Southwestern Historical Quarterly*, Vol. XXXVII, No. 2, October 1933, 116-135.

Burchardt, Bill. "Overland Mail Centennial." *Oklahoma Today Magazine*, Fall 1958.

Conrad, Judy. "Final Voyage." *American History Illustrated*, Vol. XXVI, No. 1, March/April 1991, 58-65, 72.

Crimmins, Col. Martin L. "The Stage Lines of the Southwest." *Frontier Times*, Vol. 18, No. 9, June 1941, 418-421.

Daly, Henry W. "A Dangerous Dash Down Lancaster Hill." *Frontier Times*, Vol. 30, No. 2, (April, May, June 1953), 166-173.

Davy, Dava McGahee. "The Pinery Station. Guadalupe Mountains National Park, Texas." Carlsbad Caverns Natural History Association. Carlsbad, N.M. 1977.

Duffen, William A. Editor. "Overland Via 'Jackass Mail' in 1858. The Diary of Phocion R. Way." *Arizona and the West*, Vol. 2, Nos. 1 through 4, Spring 1960 (35-53), Summer 1960 (147-164), Autumn 1960 (279-292), Winter 1960 (353-370).

Duncan, S. Blackwell. "The Legendary Concords." *The American West*, Vol. VIII, No. 1, January 1971, 16-17, 61-62.

Fauntleroy, J. D. "Old Stage Routes of Texas." *Frontier Times*, Vol. 6, No. 10, July 1929, 420-423.

Greenwood, C. L., contributed by. "Opening Routes to El Paso, 1849. Report of Dr. John S. Ford, upon the practicability of a route from Austin to El Paso del Norte." The Texas State Historical Ass'n, October 1944, No. 2, 262-271.

Herndon, John Hunter. "Diary of a Young Man in Houston, 1838." Andrew Forrest Muir, Editor. *The Southwestern Historical Quarterly*, Vol. LIII, 1949-1950.

Holden, W. C. "Law and Lawlessness on the Texas Frontier, 1875-1890." *The Southwestern Historical Quarterly*, Vol. XLIV, No. 2, October 1940, 188-203.

Hollon, W. Eugene. "Great Days of the Overland Stage." *American Heritage*, Vol. VIII, No. 4, June 1957.

Hulbert, Archer Butler, Editor. "Letters of an Overland Mail Agent in Utah. Hiram S. Rumfield Correspondence." American Antiquarian Society, Proceedings, Vol. 38, No. 2, October 17, 1928.

Hunter, J. Marvin. "Thirty-day Mail Schedule to California." *Frontier Times*, Vol. 26, No. 9, June 1949, 219-221.

Hunter, J. Marvin, Ed. "Tragedies of the Old Stage Days." *Frontier Times*, Vol. 28, No. 4, January 1951, 102-108.

Judd, Ira. "The Overland Mail." *Arizona Highways*, October 1958, 8-13, 38-39.

Mahon, Emmie Giddings W. and Chester V. Kielman. "George H. Giddings and the San Antonio-San Diego Mail Line." *The Southwestern Historical Quarterly*, Vol. LXI, No. 2, October 1957, 220-239.

McChristian, Douglas C. "Apaches and Soldiers: Mail Protection in West Texas." Periodical: *The Journal of the Council on America's Military Past*, XIII:3, 3-17.

Myres, Sanda L., Editor. "A Woman's View of the Texas Frontier, 1874: The Diary of Emily K. Andrews." *Southwestern Historical Quarterly*, Vol. LXXXVI, No. 1, July 1982, 49-80.

"Narratives of the First Trip from San Antonio, Texas to El Paso, Mexico." *Appleton's Journal of Literature, Science & Art*, Vol. 4, December 1870, 702-704, 738-740.

Newsom, W. L. "The Postal System of the Republic of Texas." *The Southwestern Historical Quarterly*, Vol. XX, No. 2, October 1916.

Pappas, Joann V., Editor. "The Irregular Mail of the Texas Republic." *Star of the Republic Museum Notes*, Vol. IV, No. 4, Summer 1980.

Richardson, Rupert N. "Some Details of the Southern Overland Mail." *The Southwestern Historical Quarterly*, Vol. XXIX, No. 1, July 1925, 1-18.

Schmidt, Stephen H., Editor. "Fort Concho 1868-1872: The Medical Officer's Observations by William M. Notson." *Military History of Texas and the Southwest*, Vol. 12, 125-149.

Smith, Ophia D. "A Trip to Texas in 1855." *The Southwestern Historical Quarterly*, Vol. LIX, No. 1, July 1955, 24-39.

"Tells of Depredations of Early Day Robber." San Angelo *Times*, in *Frontier Times*, Vol. 6, No. 10, July 1929, 423-424.

Waring, Katharine T. Fort Concho Report, Vol. 18, No. 4, Winter 1986-1987, 30-34.

Weddle, Robert S. "The Pegleg Stage Robbers." *Southwest Heritage*, Vol. 3, No. 2, March 1969, 2-9.

Williams, J. W. "The Butterfield Overland Mail Road Across
Texas." *The Southwestern Historical Quarterly*, Vol. LXI, No. 1,
July 1957, 1-19.
Wynes, Charles E., Editor. "Lewis Harvie Blair: Texas Travels,
1851-1855." *The Southwestern Historical Quarterly*, Vol. LXVI,
No. 2, October 1962, 262-266.

NEWSPAPERS

Missouri *Republican*
New York *Daily Times*
Omaha *Herald*
Press-Argus Centennial Edition
Sacramento *Union*
St. Joseph *Catholic Tribune*
San Antonio *Express / Daily Express*
San Antonio *Herald / Daily Herald*
San Francisco *Bulletin*
San Francisco *Call*
Sherman *Democrat*

BOOKS

Armes, Col. George A. *Ups and Downs of an Army Officer*.
Washington, D.C. 1900.
Austerman, Wayne R. *Sharps Rifles and Spanish Mules. The
San Antonio-El Paso Mail, 1851-1881*. Texas A&M University
Press, College Station TX., 1985.
Banning, Capt. William and George Hugh Banning. *Six Horses*. The
Century Co., New York, 1928.
Barnes, Demas. *From the Atlantic to the Pacific, Overland*. D. Van
Nostrand, New York, 1866. Reprint, Ray A. Billington, Editor,
Arno Press, New York, 1973.
Barrows, H. D. "A Two Thousand Mile Stage Ride." From *The First
Overland Mail*, Walter B. Lang. Roycrofters, East Aurora, New
York, 1945.
Boggs, Mae Helene Bacon. *My Playhouse Was A Concord Coach. An
Anthology of Newspaper Clippings and Documents Relating to
Those Who Made California History During the Years 1822-1888*.
Howell-North Press, Oakland CA, 1942.

Branda, Eldon Stephen, Editor. *The Handbook of Texas*. Vol. III, The Texas State Historical Ass'n, Austin, 1976.

Carter, Kathryn Turner. *Stagecoach Inns of Texas*. Texian Press, Waco TX, 1972.

Carter, R. G. Capt. *On The Border With Mackenzie*. Antiquarian Press, Ltd., NY, 1961.

Conkling, Roscoe P. and Margaret B. Conkling. *The Butterfield Overland Mail, 1857-1869. Its organization and operation over the Southern Route to 1861; subsequently over the Central Route to 1866; and under Wells, Fargo and Company in 1869*. Three Volumes. The Arthur H. Clark Co., Glendale CA, 1947.

Conger, Roger N., James M. Day, Joe B. Frantz, et al. *Frontier Forts of Texas*. Texian Press, Waco TX, 1966.

Dietrich, Wilfred O. *The Blazing Story of Washington County*. Banner Press, Brenham TX, 1950.

Dunbar, Seymour. *A History of Travel in America: Being an Outline in Modes of Travel . . . . Archaic Vehicles . . . . Colonial Times to the Completion of the First Transcontinental Railroad: Influence of . . . . Indians on the Free Movement and Territorial Unity of . . . . White Race: Travel Methods: Related Human Experiences . . . . Growth of a National Travel System*. Tudor Publishing Co., New York, 1937.

Dunlop, Richard. *Wheels West, 1590-1900*. Rand McNally & Co., New York, 1977.

Duval, John C. *The Adventures of Big-Foot Wallace*. University of Nebraska Press, Lincoln, 1936. Editors: Mabel Major and Rebecca Smith Lee.

Eggenhofer, Nick. *Wagons, Mules and Men. How the Frontier Moved West*. Hastings House Publishers, New York, 1961.

Ford, Worthington C., Editor. *The Writings of Washington*. Fourteen Volumes. Vol. 2 (pp 290- 292), New York, 1889-1893.

Foster-Harris. *The Look of the Old West*. Bonanza Books, NY, 1960.

Froebel, Julius. *Seven Years' Travel in Central America, Northern Mexico, and the Far West of the United States*. Richard Bentley, London, 1859.

Gard, Wayne, Dean Krakel, Joe B. Frantz, et al. *Along the Early Trails of the Southwest*. The Pemberton Press, Jenkins Publishing Co., Austin & New York, 1969.

Gillett, James B. *Six Years With the Texas Rangers. 1875 to 1881*. Yale University Press, New Haven, 1925.

Hafen, LeRoy R. *The Overland Mail, 1849-1869: Promoter of Settlement, Precursor of Railroads*. The Arthur H. Clark Co., Cleveland, 1926.

_____ , W. Eugene Hollon, and Carl Coke Rister. *Western America. The Exploration, Settlement and Development of the Region Beyond the Mississippi.* Prentice-Hall, Inc., Englewood Cliffs NJ, 1970.

Haines, Francis. *Horses in America.* Thomas Y. Crowell Co., New York, 1971.

Hart, Herbert M. *Old Forts of the Southwest.* Bonanza Books, New York, 1974.

Holmes, Oliver W., and Peter T. Rohrbach. *Stagecoach East. Stagecoach Days in the East from the Colonial Period to the Civil War.* Smithsonian Institution Press, Washington, D.C., 1983.

Hornung, Clarence P. *Wheels Across America. A pictorial cavalcade illustrating the early development of vehicular transportation.* A.S. Barnes & Co., New York, 1959.

Houstonn, Mrs. E. M. *Texas and The Gulf of Mexico; or, Yachting in the New World.* John Murray, London, 1844. Reprint, with Introduction by Dorman H. Winfrey, Steck-Warlick Co., Austin TX, 1968.

Krueger, Max Amadeus Paulus. *Second Fatherland. The Life and Fortunes of a German Immigrant.* Texas A&M University Press, College Station TX, 1976.

Kelley, Dayton. *Handbook of Waco and McLennan County, Texas.* Texian Press, Waco TX, 1972.

Lang, Walter Barnes. *The First Overland Mail: Butterfield Trail. St. Louis to San Francisco, 1858-1861.* Walter B. Lang, 1940.

_____. *The First Overland Mail: Butterfield Trail. San Francisco to Memphis, 1858-1861.* Walter B. Lang, 1945.

Ledbetter, Barbara A. Neal. *Fort Belknap. Frontier Saga.* Eakin Press, Burnet TX, 1982.

Lesley, Lewis Burt. *Uncle Sam's Camels.* Harvard University Press, Cambridge, 1929.

Lucas, Mattie Davis and Mita H. Hall. *A History of Grayson County, Texas.* Sherman, 1936.

McConnell, H. H. *Five Years A Cavalryman; or, Sketches of Regular Army Life on the Texas Frontier, Twenty Odd Years Ago.* J.N. Rogers & Co., Printers, Jacksboro TX, 1889.

Mills, Anson. *My Story.* Press of Byron S. Adams, Washington, D.C., 1918.

Mills, W. W. *Forty Years at El Paso. 1858-1898.* Carl Hertzog, El Paso TX, 1962.

Moody, Ralph. *Stagecoach West.* Thomas Y. Crowell Co., New York, 1967.

Moore Sr., Ben. *Butterfield: Seven Years With The Wild Indians.* Ben Moore, Sr., O'Donnell TX, 1945.

Mountfield, David. *The Coaching Age.* Robert Hale & Co., London, 1976.

Mullin, Robert N. *Stagecoach Pioneers of the Southwest.* Southwestern Studies, Monograph No. 71, Texas Western Press, University of Texas at El Paso, 1983.

Murray, Amelia M. *Letters from the United States, Cuba and Canada.* G.P. Putnam & Co., 1856. Reprint, Negro Universities Press, New York, 1969.

Nevin, David. *The Expressmen.* The Old West Series, Time-Life Books, 1974.

Olmsted, Frederick Law. *A Journey Through Texas, Or, a Saddle-Trip on the Southwestern Frontier.* Reprint of 1857 edition, University of Texas Press, Foreword by Larry McMurtry, Austin TX, 1978.

Ormsby, Waterman L. *The Butterfield Overland Mail.* Editors: Lyle H. Wright & Josephine M. Bynum, The Huntington Library, San Marino CA, 1954.

Paddock, Capt. B. B., Editor. *History of Texas: Fort Worth and the Texas Northwest Edition.* The Lewis Publishing Co., Chicago & New York, 1922, Vol. II.

Palmer, Richard F. *The 'Old Line Mail.' Stagecoach Days in Upstate New York.* North Country Books, Lakemont NY, 1977.

Parramore, Dock Dilworth. *Scenes and Stories of Early West Texas.* Texas Western Press, University of Texas at El Paso, 1975.

Pumpelly, Raphael. *Across America and Asia.* Leypoldt & Holt, New York, 1870.

Raht, Carlysle Graham. *The Romance of Davis Mountains and Big Bend Country.* The Rahtbooks Co., Odessa TX, 1963.

Richardson, Albert D. *Beyond the Mississippi: From the Great River to the Great Ocean.* American Publishing Co., A. Roman & Co., San Francisco CA, 1873.

Richardson, Rupert Norval. *Texas, the Lone Star State.* Prentice-Hall, Inc., Englewood Cliffs NJ, 1958.

_____. *The Frontier of Northwest Texas, 1846-1876. Advance and Defense by the Pioneer Settlers of the Cross Timbers and Prairies.* The Arthur H. Clark Co., Glendale CA, 1963.

Rister, Carl Coke. *The Southwestern Frontier — 1865-1881.* The Arthur H. Clark Co., Cleveland, 1928.

Rock, James L., and W. I. Smith. *Southern and Western Texas Guide for 1878.* A. H. Granger, St. Louis MO, 1878.

Roemer, Dr. Ferdinand. *Texas with Particular Reference to German Immigration and the Physical Appearance of the Country.* Translated from the German by Oswald Mueller. Standard Printing Co., San Antonio TX, 1935.

Root, Frank A., and William Elsey Connelley. *The Overland Stage to California. Personal Reminiscences and Authentic History of the Great Overland Stage Line and Pony Express from the Missouri River to the Pacific Ocean.* Topeka KS, 1901.

Santleben, August. *A Texas Pioneer. Early Staging and Overland Freighting Days on the Frontier of Texas and Mexico.* I. D. Affleck, Editor. The Neale Publishing Co., New York, 1910.

Scobee, Barry. *Old Fort Davis.* The Naylor Co., San Antonio TX, 1947.

Sibley, Marilyn McAdams. *Travelers in Texas, 1761-1860.* University of Texas Press, Austin, 1967.

Smithwick, Noah. *The Evolution of a State.* The Steck Co., Austin TX, 1935. A facsimile reproduction of the original *The Evolution of a State, or, Recollections of Old Texas Days,* Gammel Book Co., Austin TX, 1900.

Stambaugh, J. Lee, and Lilian J. Stambaugh. *A History of Collin County, Texas.* The Texas State Historical Ass'n, Austin, 1958.

Tallack, William. *The California Overland Express. The Longest Stage-Ride in the World.* Historical Society of Southern California, Los Angeles, Special Publication No. 1, 1935.

Taylor, Alva. *Taylor's History and Photographs of Corsicana and Navarro County.* Travis Printing Co., Corsicana TX, 1959. In Kathryn Carter, *Stagecoach Inns of Texas.*

Taylor, Morris F. *First Mail West. Stagecoach Lines on the Santa Fe Trail.* University of New Mexico Press, Albuquerque NM, 1971.

Taylor, Col. Nathaniel Alston. *The Coming Empire, or, Two Thousand Miles in Texas on Horseback.* Turner Co., Dallas TX, 1936.

Texas in 1840, or the Emigrant's Guide to the New Republic. Introduction by Rev. A.B. Lawrence. William W. Allen, New York, 1840.

Thompson, George A. *Throw Down the Box!* Dream Garden Press, Salt Lake City, Utah, 1989.

Tucker, Dr. Joseph C. *To the Golden Goal and Other Sketches.* William Doxey, San Francisco, 1895.

Twain, Mark. *Roughing It.* Grosset & Dunlap, New York, 1913.

Utley, Robert M. *Fort Davis National Historic Site, Texas.* National Park Service Historical Handbook Series No. 38, Washington D.C., 1965.

_____. *Frontiersmen in Blue. The United States Army and the Indian, 1848-1865.* The Macmilllan Co., New York, 1967.

Watkins, Sue; Editor. *One League to Each Wind. Accounts of Early Surveying in Texas.* A Publication of Texas Surveyors Ass'n, Von-Boeckmann-Jones, Printers, Austin TX, 1964.

Webb, Walter P., and Joe Bailey Carroll, Editors. *The Handbook of Texas.* Two Volumes. The Texas State Historical Ass'n, Austin, 1952.

White, Owen. *Out of the Desert. The Historical Romance of El Paso.* The McMath Co., El Paso TX, 1923.

Williams, Clayton W. *Texas' Last Frontier. Fort Stockton & the Trans-Pecos, 1861-1895.* Ernest Wallace, Editor. Texas A&M University Press, College Station TX, 1982.

Williams, J. W. *Old Texas Trails.* Eakin Press, Burnet TX, 1979.

Williams, Judge O. W. *In Old New Mexico, 1879-1880.* Fort Stockton TX, No date.

Winther, Oscar Osburn. *The Transportation Frontier. Trans-Mississippi West, 1865-1890.* Holt, Rinehart & Winston, New York, 1964.

_____. *Via Western Express & Stagecoach.* Stanford University Press, California, 1945.

UNPUBLISHED MANUSCRIPTS

McChristian, Douglas C. "Incidents Involving Hostile Indians Within the Influence of Fort Davis, Texas, 1866-1891." September 9, 1975.

Index